# SATURDAY WALK

# Saturday
# WALK

### and other stories

## JUDITH DAVIDSON CHASEK

Bridge Books

Printed in the United States of America

Bridge Books
bridgebooks.online

LCCN: 2024915057
ISBN: 979-8-9905385-0-4

# Contents

# Foreword

Max Davidson. Five foot three. Bright blue eyes. Shiny bald head. Round belly. Died before the internet was born, but you can still google him. Long-time rabbi of Congregation Beth Mordecai in Perth Amboy, New Jersey. Bigger than Perth Amboy though. President of the U.S Rabbinical Assembly, while President of the Synagogue Council of America (which brought together the three major branches of Judaism—Reformed, Conservative, Orthodox). In charge of Jewish chaplains in the U.S. military during World War II. The photo of him shaking President Harry Truman's hand. Two PhDs even though you wouldn't even know he had any, being his granddaughters who mostly associated him with ice cream at Howard Johnsons, anywhere one could be found along the Garden State Parkway between NY and NJ. Yes, we still use his old World War II haggadahs during Passover, which come to think of it, he may have had a hand in writing. When we were teenagers we were most impressed with the fact that he had reviewed Alan Ginsberg's *Kaddish* for the local newspaper, and still had it on his desk.

But this book isn't about Max Davidson the big man (although extremely short). It is about Max Davidson, the father and family man. Max was married to Margaret Kussy

Davidson, the petite, beautiful, and stylish daughter of a Newark dentist, who inherited a propensity for giggling with her 2 sisters, Sylvia and Dottie, which must have had a genetic component, as it was passed down to her two daughters, Judy and Dorie, and then to their daughters, Ruth, Margie, and Jenine. Margaret was shy, which made the job of *rebbetzin* (rabbi's wife) a difficult one, as it involved a lot of social functions, such as hosting weddings in their apartment, meeting and greeting congregants at services and social events, and engaging with the sisterhood. She had originally wanted to be a concert pianist, an inclination she promptly dropped after she married and took on the role of her lifetime—supporting and loving Max and their two children. Nervous and anxious by nature, the job was not a natural one for her, and it took its toll.

This book is also, of course, about Judy and her relationship with Max. Was he her Pygmalion? Who and what would she have been if she hadn't been his daughter? Max and Margaret had had a son as a first born, who died before he was one of some kind of pulmonary disease. When Judy came next they hired a wet nurse to breastfeed her, as apparently the lack of breastfeeding with the son had something to do with his vulnerability to disease. They never spoke about the son. But they poured everything they could into Judy and her development, and six years later, in a more relaxed way, into Dorie. As a result, Judy became an over- achiever, hosting a radio show, heading the school newspaper, a Phi Beta Kappa in college. And one who could take on her father in any intellectual debate at the kitchen table.

Judy was our mother. Because she had been so shaped and molded by her father, she took a hands off approach with us. School? Never mentioned it. Grades? I am not sure she actually looked at report cards, or if we had any. Hebrew school? One "no" was enough to scuttle the idea forever. Supervision? We mainly roamed the backyard woods on our own all day, and circled the oval around the front of the house on our bicycles endlessly, while our mother banged away at the typewriter upstairs in her den, busy writing who-knows-what.

The "who-knows-what" is this book. Judy published many short stories and articles in her life (she died of brain lymphoma at age 61). She had stints of working at magazines and newspapers (Good Housekeeping, Stamford Advocate), and stints of creating on her own as a freelance writer. In putting this anthology of her short stories together here, we focused on what seemed to be the theme she returned to again and again—her relationship with her father, the development of an independent identity away from her father, and her relationship to Judaism. She was raised in an observant household, although Max seemed to be a man with at least one foot firmly planted in the secular world. They kept kosher, didn't pass money or ride in vehicles on the Sabbath, and refrained from work (except for rabbinical work) on the Sabbath. This caused dislocation and isolation for Judy as she got older, and found she wasn't able to partake with her friends in social activities, such as taking the bus to the big high school football game on Saturdays. Her parents sent her cans of kosher meatballs when she went to college, until she eventually discarded keeping kosher and other Jewish observances.

Yet, yet. We never missed a high holiday service—this being the only time we ever went to services, we felt like nervous strangers when we sat in the suburban palace of a synagogue, looking at the well-dressed people around us (we usually had holes in our tights), the experience devoid of any drop of spirituality. Finally, Judy and Norman (her engineer/inventor husband) found a small *havurah* that met in the cafeteria of a local school, and they re-engaged, somewhat, and on their own non-observant terms, with Judaism again. However, all of her involvement in social justice movements throughout her life were based on her Jewish values.

Judy dropped the idea of being a superstar too, at least outwardly. As she notes ironically in "Wives and Daughters" her mentor/father seemed to drop these expectations too, once she got married. Our memories focus around sitting in a big pile with her on the couch, where we discussed anything at all, giggled, and felt safe, loved, and listened to. She never mentioned her ambitions, and never seemed disappointed in her life, although she did let us know that she would have rather lived in a city, or at least downtown, than down a dirt road in semi-rural Connecticut.

In publishing this book, we hope to share with others these funny, observant, and perceptive stories, which define a life, a time, and the ongoing struggle to define who we are as individuals.

Ruth Chasek and Marjorie Chasek Sweet

# 1

# The Hoopa Holder

Where is it now, I wonder, that old hoopa of maroon velvet, the marriage canopy held up by four poles? It was our job—my mother's, sister's and mine—to hold up the hoopa whenever a wedding was performed in our home.

At "weddings in the rabbi's home" our services were indispensable. We knew, of course, that more formal weddings were held at the Temple on Sundays, with long white dresses and flower girls and hors d'oeuvres. These irritated us because they were often the reason that Daddy must cancel a planned drive to the seashore or a huckleberrying jaunt to Cheesequake Park. We knew, too, that some weddings were held in the "rabbi's study" at the Temple, but these sounded too makeshift and perfunctory to deserve mention (imagine a wedding in a study!) and anyhow, we always wondered who held the hoopa there.

As an official hoopa-holder (with several auxiliary functions such as glass-filler and cake-passer) I participated in hundreds of home weddings as a child. Sometimes these were expected for weeks; sometimes we would be unexpectedly routed out of bed in the dead of night and would grope for the hoopa pole with eyes full of sleepers. Some of the weddings were large affairs, to my mother's horror. ("A wedding that big should be at the Temple!" she would tell my father.) She was shy, and no hostess, and even the wine and cake served at these functions taxed her catering talents to the limit. I remember one afternoon when 100 guests unexpectedly showed up for a wedding in our small apartment: guests spilled over into the bathroom and dangled their legs from our bathtub, munching wine and cake. On the other hand, some weddings were so small that there were not even enough witnesses to make it legal, and Buddy Spitz would have to be summoned from the apartment downstairs.

There were variations through the years in our musical fare also. During one period we owned a piano, and my mother would bang out Lohengrin's Wedding March on the piano while the bride (in a brown wool going away dress) marched from one end of our living room to the other—a distance of about 8 feet, but we thought it chic. There was another period, after the piano had been sold, when we played the Wedding March on the record player. This era came to an abrupt end one June day when I was ten. I was then in the process of amassing a record collection, consisting mostly of those nasal, nauseating numbers popular with the pre-teen set. A pile of our records lay on the phonograph table. It was one of the larger weddings. The last nervous cough had subsided. My father, prayer book in hand, was poised beneath the hoopa. The bride began moving down our home-made aisle. It was a touching, trembly moment. At a nod from Dad, my sister Dorie grabbed a record and inserted the needle, and the bride walked to her groom to the raucous rhythms of the popular hit, "I'm a Big Girl Now."

The pre-wedding preparations would begin in the parlor before the guests arrived. The hoopa, disassembled and collapsed, would be pulled out from its place behind the filing cabinet in the parlor. Then Dorie and I would help my father put it all together (each of the four poles consisted of two parts, which must be screwed together.) Sometimes I suspected that this was the part of the wedding which my father, who loved gadgets, relished most. (He later became a camera bug, and a fancier of silex coffee pots.)

And there it would suddenly bloom in the middle of our plain, modest living room… an elegant, sumptuous hoopa of heavy maroon velvet, worthy of getting married under. Immediately a very special mood—festive, ceremonious— began to pervade the room.

It was rather dull for the first few minutes after the guests arrived. There was much official business to be attended to at the dining room table—kesubas to be signed, documents to be read and sworn to. My father, suddenly attired in skullcap and spectacles, would be sitting in the big French chair at the dining room table inquiring into middle initials and dates of birth. Invariably there was the awkward pause when the bride groom "couldn't quite recollect" what his name was in Hebrew—a mortified mama would be summoned to provide it, along with an embarrassed explanation: "Rabbi, you just can't imagine what a marvelous Bar Mitzvah boy Yitzhawk was, but he just forgets today, he's so excited." Sometimes, to our delight, some hitherto hidden fact would come to light during these dry legal exercises—such as, that the groom had already been married three times before, or the bride wasn't Jewish—and cause a stir of scandal and excitement. But generally this official period was a dull one and Dorie and I would pass around the sponge cake and honey cake and take a few sips of cordial if no one was looking.

Then there would be the nervous scrambling for places under the hoopa, my father instructing everyone on where he should stand. The electricity that passed through the room at this point communicated itself even to children and professional hoopa-holders. Mom, Dorie and I immediately scrambled to our posts, behind our respective hoopa poles, and a fourth person was enlisted to hold up the remaining pole. The ceremony began.

The ceremony was full of lovely rhythms and cadences and fine dramatic touches (my father was a master of these, was famous for them). We loved it when the bride's mother lifted the veil off her daughter's face and tenderly fed her a drop of wine, putting the goblet to her lips just as if she were still a child—to symbolize, my father would explain, the years of parental care and preparation that had preceded this ceremony. And we liked it when the bride fed the groom a drop of wine, and the groom did likewise, "to represent," my father said, "the first food shared as husband and wife under their first roof" (the hoopa).

And when he boomed,

*"By virtue of the authority in me—vested by the laws of the State of New Jersey,*

*By virtue of the authority in me—vested as an ordained rabbi in Israel,*

*I now pronounce..."*

We were thrilled and impressed, no matter how many times we heard it.

But unfortunately, my mother comes from a long line of gigglers.

My mother and her sisters had been notorious in Newark. They erupted at Friday night services; they exploded at Bar Mitzvahs; Thanksgiving dinners at their home were orgies of hilarity. Still they could be seen every Monday at Shraffts, chattering and giggling for hours over their grilled cheese sandwiches—over the trouble Sylvia had had exchanging a bra at Bamberger's, or over one of Dotty's inimitable mimicries. The more solemn the occasion, the more irrepressible the giggle—and Dorie and I, alas, had inherited the fatal affliction.

Weddings were no exception. At the most sober and significant moment, when the hush was deepest, my mother's eyes would meet mine over the sea of veils and feathers and skullcaps, and we would be off.

It took little to set us off—the bridegroom picking his nose, the bride's mother yanking at her girdle, and we quickly ignited each other and then Dorie.

You cannot possibly imagine the desperate, agonizing sensation of trying to gulp down the giggle rising inexorably in our throats. I must not, I would tell myself, I simply must not, I can not, digging my fingernails into my palms and grasping the hoopa pole harder. But the more acutely we realized how unthinkable it was, the stronger grew the impulse.

If nipped in an incipient stage—by a sidelong glance from my father or a certain hardening of his voice during the Boo-ray-Ott Mikoodeshus, discernible only to us—it was sometimes possible to pass off the giggle as a cough, or, better yet, as a sob. This latter was positively commendable and brought appreciative glances from sobbing tantas and uncles who felt that the rabbi's family really cared.

Usually, however, this was impossible; the giggle would burst forth from all three sides of the hoopa; the hoopa would start to pitch and heave; and only the steadying efforts of the fourth hoopa-holder (some frowning cousin of the bride) prevented it from coming down on the heads of all the bemused principals. I suppose that's why God made hoopas with 4 poles.

Eventually we subsided, blushing furiously. The wedding went on, and at last the ceremony reached its dramatic crescendo: the bridegroom's smashing a glass jar with his foot, commemorating the smashing of the temple in Jerusalem ("because," my father explained, "we Jews always inject a note of sadness into even our happiest moments.") I could never quite grasp this, but it was a handy way of disposing of our old mayonnaise jars, and it did conclude the evening in a dramatic way.

Then there were the huggings and mazel tovs, and after another taste of wine and cake, the wedding party would disappear. Years later Dorie and I would spot the bride on Smith Street, pushing a baby carriage.

That was how weddings were to me until I turned 14 and was suddenly, out of the blue, in one—a fancy one, my cousin's, and I was cast as maid of honor, descending a winding staircase in a full-length yellow lace gown. I stood beneath the hoopa, and passed the glass of wine to my cousin, and the hoopa was made of green vines, and directly after the ceremony—I don't recall how or why—a dark, handsome sailor named Pav whom I had never seen before, and was never to see again, grabbed me and kissed me directly on the lips. It was my first kiss. It was a marvelous kiss. Perhaps I held up our hoopa after that, with Mom and Dorie, but I was never to see a wedding in the same way again.

# 2

# Inventing the
# Sewing Machine

I t was shortly after seeing the movie *Young Tom Edison* that I invented the sewing machine. It came to me in a flash. The idea of the sewing machine, very much in the manner that Tom had gotten his ideas.

That movie had been a devastating experience. I wept and laughed with Tom sharing his every defeat and triumph—being jeered at by the children and cast out of school just for exploding gunpowder in the schoolhouse corridors in a well-meant experiment; an ingenious maze of pulleys that he rigged up lifting the shades all over the house; being jeered and spat on by his fellow students and chased up a tree merely for being odd; the long hours in the cellar tinkering with bells and signals and pulleys; his mother bringing apple pie and milk to his workbench surreptitiously because his father sternly disapproved of the foolish boy; that splendid moment when he stopped two trains from colliding by working the telegraph signal—all of it I watched breathlessly and while the sheer adventure was thrilling it was something entirely new that shook me to my foundations as I watched. lt was my first glimpse of genius.

For weeks after seeing Young Tom Edison (and I saw it three times) I filled up notebook after notebook just retelling the story as fiction: "Then Tommy woke up and..."

Tom made her shade go up with his rope and the shades flew up. "And as I scribbled I identified more and more with the abused and misunderstood genius. In the criticism of my friends ("Spoil sport—It's my turn bouncing!") I began to perceive the persecution of the gifted. In my father's every disapproving remark ("For god's sake Judy, elbows off the table!") I thought I discerned the parental opaqueness associated with the unworthy parents of genius. And then one morning when I awoke I had it in a flash—the idea of the Sewing Machine.

My total unfamiliarity with the rudiments of sewing, even by hand, did not deter me at all. Indeed it was an advantage, since I was not held back by old fangled methodology. I saw it all—a maze of pulleys and loops and strings which when all manipulated together just so would completely do away with the humdrum work of hand sewing. Hereafter a machine would do the work.

I rounded up a small table, many loops of clothesline, and 15 spools of multicolored thread. Nearby lay my mother's sewing basket full of needles and pins.

"Mom could you please get me some apple pie and milk?"

Alas there was only sponge cake in the house but after much pleading my mother promised to purchase apple pie the following day at the supermarket when made to understand its function on my creative faculties. For three days I locked myself in my room constructing great pulleys intertwined with multicolored threads. From time to time my mother would enter the room quietly, meekly respectful of genius, and quite impressed with the growing superstructure of rope, pulleys, threads, and needles.

I listened eagerly for some disapproving growls from my father to the effect that I must be addled to hole up like that with my invention, but disappointingly he too sounded a bit impressed when he peeked, tiptoed away, and said to my mother in the kitchen, "I can't tell what it is, Margaret, but it certainly is something." In fact I began to hear a suppressed awe in his voice.

Finally my machine was completed. The table was a complex and dizzying maze of loops and pulleys with threads keeping parts of the rope together. I stared at it in admiration. Now there was only one thing more—I must figure out just how it was to sew.

To this problem I had as yet given only the scantest attention, so far busy constantly with the machine. Now, just how was the machine to go about sewing? I gathered some ripped clothes and placed them firmly on the busy table under the system of ropes and threads. Now then, how would it work?

"Mother," I called out, "Could I please have some more apple pie and milk?"

Eagerly, just like Tom's mother, my mother came running in with a fresh slice of apple pie and milk. The refrigerator was kept stocked daily now.

"Dear, how are you ?"

"Mother! Please, can't you see I'm thinking?"

Aghast, my mother clapped her hand over her mouth and vanished. Now I had to make it work. A bite of apple pie and I had it! An inspiration from on high, just like Tom.

My machine would have two needles instead of the one used in hand sewing! That would mean the machine would sew twice as fast as hand. Yes, two needles that was it. I would attach two needles to a pulley system so that when the rope was pulled just once, it would set in motion two needles. What a worksaver, just like Tom's pulleys! Overwhelmed by my own brilliance I eagerly attached two needles to one pulley and gazed admiringly at my handiwork. Now then, how was the thing to sew? And here, alas, I was stuck.

How was it to sew? It was the one point I couldn't work out. The machine itself, its elaborate network of pulleys and threads, had been clear as a bell and indeed it was an impressive specimen. But to make it sew—that was a stopper.

I attached a foot pedal to one of the clothesline pulleys to see what happened. Tom always had to try out all kinds of chemicals, didn't he, before getting the right mixture? When I stepped on the pedal the pulley moved, yes? And that made the two needles move too because they were attached to the pulley. But alas nothing sewed. The machine wouldn't sew. And try as I would, think as I might, devour plate after plate of apple pie and milk as I would, I couldn't make that darn contraption sew. I did however contract a serious belly ache from all that pie, which put me to bed for several days. I lay there, the baffling contraption still rigged up across the room. Finally a friend came to visit and spied it.

"What on earth is that?"

I thought with relief, just like Tom. I too would experience the contempt of one's contemporaries. But disappointingly she was rather sympathetic and interested when I told her I was inventing a machine to sew.

"Oh really, A machine to sew, Why?"

"What do you mean why? It will save millions of people drudging hours of work with their hands and free them for other things."

"Oh, but what's wrong with the sewing machines we have now?"

"The What?"

"The sewing machines we have now."

And she told me. She told me that the sewing machine had already been invented. Her own mother had one. At first I refused to believe it. But finally the whole awful truth sunk in. Someone else, many years ago, had invented a sewing machine.

For a while I was heartsick. There was a short time even when I doubted whether I was destined for genius. However when I got out of bed and went to my friend's house I had a thrill that revived my prospects.

Her sewing machine had two needles.

Hmmm, I told myself, the two needle idea was the basis of the sewing machine now used. But hadn't I thought it up independently myself? Surely that was a sign of originality or even more. Coming home that day I called out, "Ma, can I have some apple pie and milk?"

# 3

# The Korbins

The first time I ever saw a Korbin was when I had the measles. Having wearied of the library books, jigsaw puzzles, and homemade puppets strewn about the bed I had glanced out the backyard window. What I saw there startled me.

A little boy about 9 was making off with my bike. He had gone into the garage and was now driving off on it looking furtively to the right and left to make sure no one was looking.

I blinked. The whole thing seemed like a fantasy all mixed up with the fever and the red blotches and the itches.

On State Street there was not the community of property feeling that exists sometimes in garden apartments and developments where the toys are all sort of lumped together out on the sidewalk. On State Street the houses were separated from each other by tall ugly hedges. People didn't just come and borrow your toys without asking.

Of course I had read about stealing in all of those books I voraciously devoured. The mysteries were full of them and The Shadow was always catching crooks on Sunday night. Somehow I immediately lumped this act with them. There was something about the way the boy had glanced furtively about him that joined him inextricably with the crooks and thieves of the books. This was no kid taking a ride on another kid's bike. This was a thief. A thief. Something out of my ken—entirely, utterly strange. I felt a little thrill.

"Mommy!" I cried. "There's a boy stealing my bicycle." My mother came running.

"What do you mean stealing your bike?"

"He's gone now. He just took it out of the garage and rode away."

"Did you see who it was?"

"I never saw him before."

"Well now don't you worry about it dear. I'll take care of it. Wait till Daddy comes home. Now you go to bed."

Evidently she thought it was a feverish imagining. But later when they thought I was asleep I heard them whispering about it in the kitchen. Evidently my father had noticed it was gone when he had parked his car.

"Now Margaret, I'm not saying they did. It's just that they just moved in yesterday and I noticed a little boy about nine. We'll just keep an eye open."

"Oh Max, you're so suspicious. It's not like a rabbi."

"Well I didn't like their looks, that's all. But I'm not saying...."

Who could they be talking of? I asked my mother the next day who had moved in.

"Oh a new family dear, the Korbins. They've got lots of children." She tried to sound happy about it but it didn't work.

I heard more mumbling in the kitchen that night and some urgent phone calls. I knew it had something to do with my bike but they were evasive when I asked them. I kept watching the back window in fascination wondering what would happen next. One day the bike suddenly reappeared in the garage. I asked my father about it. He said yes he had found it. The little boy next door had it but now it was back.

"You mean he stole it?"

"Well he just didn't understand."

"He knew it wasn't his didn't he?"

"Well he won't do it again. Now get back in bed."

I kept watching the window hoping the boy would return but he didn't. I wished I could crane my neck so as to see the house next door but I couldn't. A thief next door. I couldn't wait to see the whole family. As soon as my measles were better my curiosity was satisfied.

Why there were seven children. I counted them twice. Who ever heard of seven children? This in itself was enough to set them apart from anything I had ever known. Nobody on State Street had seven children. Betty Doctofsky had three and everyone sort of blushed when they talked about it. Everybody on State Street had two children. It was the depression and that was about all people could afford and people said this was just a nice size family. But to think that somewhere out in the world there were families of seven children. Where did they all fit? I tried to imagine them all sitting around the table at the same time. Betty, Bertha, Lucille, Jean, Bruce, Lloyd, Earl. My heavens. It was impossible. The Korbins were a curiosity.

They dressed differently too. Whereas State Street children in the summertime were practically naked, wearing just a pair of panties cut from the same material as their short little playsuits, the Korbin girls—Betty was 3, Bertha 6, Lucille 8—looked like little grown up ladies. Their dresses were made of the same material their mother wore and came down to their knees. They looked much older than us.

The girls were odd but it was the boys who scared us. Brucie, the boy who had taken the bike, was always scowling and marking up garages with chalk and things like that. But he didn't do it like he was having fun. He seemed to want to hurt us. We all felt there was something kind of sinister about the way he soaped up the car windows on Halloween. Not funny or wild, just sinister.

And there was something vaguely menacing about the big boys Earl and Lloyd, in their early teens. You couldn't put your finger on it at first. It was just that they wore tight dungarees and kept their hands in their pockets and laughed a little nastily. But that was before they started The State Street Gang.

There were plenty of little knots of friends on State Street. They played baseball together and in the summer made lemonade to sell and gave Worlds Fairs and theater productions in the garages. But this State Street Gang was different. You never really saw them, you just heard about them. Lloyd and Earl had banded together with three other toughs they had rounded up at the end of State Street and went around beating up other boys their age. Then they started on the younger boys. We had not heard of them touching a girl, but we were scared of them. When we saw them coming we always crossed the street.

"Just you don't bother with them and they won't bother with you," my mother told me. But I could tell she was a little nervous about it.

Our hearts always pounded with fear when we saw one of the State Street gang around. Some of the mothers we heard complained to their parents when their boys had been roughed up, but Mrs. Korbin always defended her boys and never punished them.

"Boys will be boys." she always said.

We were a little afraid of Mrs. Korbin herself but in a different way. We knew she wouldn't hit us or anything, but we knew she didn't like us. She was a stocky woman who looked as if she had muscles in her arms when she beat her carpets. She was always grimly busy around the house. We were glad it wasn't us she was beating. We could feel she hated us. She wore thick black stockings that made her legs look even thicker than they were.

We knew she was tough when we heard her yelling at Mr. Korbin. Mr. Korbin was the only one who seemed human. He was a timid-looking thin little man who worked setting as a linotype operator at the newspaper. We knew the boys laughed in his face when he tried to correct them. We heard her yelling hoarsely at him and suspected her of beating him up at night.

The girls did not scare us but we had little to do with them. They seemed content to stick to themselves. Our contacts were limited to occasional conversations and an occasional game of Girls Boys on the pavement.

One hot sultry noon day however I chanced to be in the backyard by myself. All my friends had gone off to summer camp. I was lonely. I had been thinking what fun it would be to have a picnic lunch in the backyard. But it wouldn't be much fun alone. Shucks. Just then I saw Lucille Korbin in her yard.

"Lucille!" I cried out on an impulse. "Let's have a picnic lunch in the backyard."

"Huh?"

I faltered, regretting the impulse. But I went on.

"You know, ask your mother to make you a picnic lunch and I will too and we'll have a picnic!"

"Okay, I'll ask my ma."

We both scooted into the house. My mother made me a sandwich. I got a little suitcase I had and put the lunch in it. It was a valise. It would be like I was traveling somewhere on a train.

Lucille wasn't ready so I waited for her. She called from her house.

"I'll be there in a few minutes, ma's still makin' it."

Lucille met me. She was carrying a small paper bag. When she saw my valise she stopped short.

"Ohhh."

"What's the matter?"

"Ohh, you brought so much. I dint know you got a big box full. I just gotta little bag, a small lunch. You gotta big one. I just got sandwiches. I didn't know we were gonna bring so much."

I laughed. "Oh no, I just put it in my valise. I just gotta sandwich too."

Uncertainly she opened her bag. She withdrew two thick sandwiches full of beef and cheese and tomato and two pieces of fruit wrapped in waxed paper and a slick of home made cake.

I opened my valise and withdrew my one peanut butter sandwich. I suddenly felt very embarrassed.

"Well y'see I told ya I didn't bring much."

I felt foolish. Here I had brought this gigantic valise and had just this paltry sandwich and she in her little paper bag had such a big lunch. I watched in fascination as she unwrapped her lunch.

"You kin have one of my sandwiches if you like," she said, feeling my discomfort.

I refused. But I was all confused. The Korbins were thieves, bullies, lowdowns. But here her mother had made her such a nice big picnic lunch, much nicer than mine. It didn't fit. I couldn't seem to put it all together. And now Lucille was offering her a piece of her sandwich. Suddenly I was all mixed up about the Korbins.

A terrible confusing thought swept through my head. Could there be something about the Korbins that I didn't know about?

# 4

# The War Effort

I just read that the people making a movie of Mary Poppins decided to set it in the 1890s instead of the 1930s because Mary Poppins is an airy childhood fantasy and the 1930s are associated with grimness.

This startled me. I was born in 1930 and the first crucial ten years of my life, those formative years, were all spent in the 1930s and I don't associate them with grimness at all. It reminds me of how my mother once disappointed me when I looked up from a Fitzgerald novel and realized with new respect that she had been of courting age in the Flaming Twenties.

"So you were a flapper, Mom?"

"No I wasn't, " she replied.

"You had a raccoon coat, didn't you?"

"Sheared beaver," was her answer.

It further developed that she could barely Charleston, had spent the better part of the Flaming Twenties typing law briefs in her Uncle Nathan's office, and the wildest thing she had done in the entire decade (she still blushed to mention it) was to kiss my father on the way home from Friday night services when they weren't even engaged. So it was with me and the Grim 1930s.

For me the Thirties stand for hopscotch and Girl-Boys, A My Name Is Anna, Miss a Bounce and Lose Your Turn, Double Dutch jump rope and the disgrace of being double-handed, Prince Valiant comic books, the Shadow, and Mary Poppins herself.

By some tour de force my parents managed to conceal the Depression from me altogether.

The Grim Thirties were followed by the War Years. This was different. I heard about the war and like many of my generation, I enjoyed it thoroughly. To me the War was Jimmy Stewart, Van Johnson, Kate Smith, "Any Bonds Today" by the Andrews Sisters, "Praise the Lord and Pass the Ammunition," and pursuing suspected spies down State Street. My first intimation of the Gathering Storm occurred on my way home from kindergarten in 1936 when a child buttonholed me and asked:

"Who you for, the Chinese or the Japanese?"

"Watcha mean?" I asked. I could tell though from the way he stared and waited expectantly that I must have some definite preference. Unfortunately I didn't.

I racked my skimpy store of oriental knowledge. Chinese children had bangs, didn't they? And Emperors with lovely artificial nightingales who sometimes didn't wear clothes. And the Japanese children had bright kimonos and laughing eyes, carrying pink parasols to keep off the sun. Which, I wondered feverishly, was I supposed to be for?

"The Japanese." I declared hastily.

"Wrong answer," he said. But this political vagueness passed. By 1941 I was breaking all the dishes in the house marked "made in Japan" with a fine patriotic flourish and hissing Japan at the Saturday afternoon movies between pops of my bubblegum.

From these Saturday movies we could see that the war was something thrilling and glamorous, full of handsome soldiers with dimpled chins kissing beautiful USO hostesses in between the battles.

Not that it was all fun though. There was our war work. We were an important part of the home front in the sixth grade when each of us knitted woolen squares for a blanket. All these little squares we were told would be sewn together to form a warm blanket for the boys at the front. We knit during class and while other girls were turning out perfect little square 6 inches by 6 inches, mine invariably turned out rectangles. Carried away by my own virtuosity I always forgot to stop in time. Moreover during arithmetic I always dropped a couple of stitches. For example, on the day they introduced fractions I dropped an entire row and as a consequence my squares had a somewhat moth-eaten look. I would place them in the converted Saltines box a little sheepishly hoping no soldier would catch a draft because of me.

But this was not our only contribution to the war effort. We pursued spies. You could always tell a spy because he carried a briefcase and wore rimless eyeglasses. Whenever we children spotted anyone of this suspicious description we followed him for hours hiding behind hedges and under porches until finally around supper time we would lose his scent.

However my major contribution to the cause of the war was my confirmation speech about Hitler at the age of 13.

Each May on Shavuot all the 13-year-old girls in the Sunday School were formally initiated as Jewesses in a colorful Confirmation ceremony at the Temple. The girls wore long white gowns—their first formals—and marched down the aisle of the Temple carrying nosegays, just like little brides. The mothers always sniffed to one another choking back tears. The Temple was always packed to the rafters for this occasion. It was one of the best shows in town every year, rivaling the annual Y Show at which Dorothy Nussbaum in black tights tap danced on the stage of the YMHA to deafening applause.

---

NOW I WAS 13 AND IT WAS MY TURN TO BE CONFIRMED. I had, to my chagrin, flunked tryouts for the Y show. My rendering of Little Sir Echo had been gratingly off key. But I was determined to make my mark at Confirmation. I would give a spectacular, a memorable performance. For years I'd been sitting in the congregation hearing my father stir the congregation to its depths with his sonorous speeches. Now I would do the same.

We were exactly ten girls this year, which delighted my father from the start—a ten-girl confirmation class happened rarely, like a full eclipse of the sun, but when it did, it meant the girls could be the Ten Commandments. And what could be more appropriate since the festival of Shevuoth commemorated the receiving of the Commandments on Sinai. Since my father rarely got a class of exactly ten girls he was always having to settle for piecemeal themes. The confirmation class just before ours—conceived at a discouraged moment right after the Stock Market Crash, had been a meager two girls, and Barbara Bruck and Elaine Filenbaum had looked awfully lonely on either side of the big pulpit declaiming on The Jewish Woman and The Jewish Home respectively. But our class—we could be commandments.

Anita Goldman drew Thou Shalt Not Murder. Natalie Gross got Adultery—the most poised member of our class she was to deliver our speech with such aplomb that no one in the audience ever guessed she hadn't the faintest notion what she was talking about. I had Thou Shalt Not Steal and was determined to do it up brown.

First came the nervous preparation of speeches. A fiction was maintained every year that the girls write their own speeches. Actually we roughed out a first draft, but my father doctored them up and they were returned to our hands with a faintly rabbinical flavor. My speech dealt with the crimes of Hitler. Then came the frenzied memorization of speeches and the Cantor's frantic last minute effort to keep us in reasonable harmony on all five verses of "Father See Thy Suppliant Children."

Mothers spent the greater part of the year rifling through dresses at Saks or Shirley Spiegels trying to locate just the gown for their daughter—something that was pious and innocently provocative at the same time.

I loathed my gown. It was marquisette and reminded me of mosquito netting. Nobody else had marquisette, I thought. None of the girls could forgive Anita Goldman for having a dress with a sweetheart neck. She was the prettiest girl anyhow and this we felt was taking unfair advantage. Never mind, I thought I would outshine them all.

The great day finally arrived. The great Temple sanctuary was thronged, dim, and echoing. Klein the Shamus was closing the great oak door—no more room. The last aunt had been to the powder room and returned. The organ sounded. One by one we trailed down the long aisle and took our seats on the pulpit. Edie Kaplowitz, flawless and breathless, delivered her speech about Honoring Father and

Mother. Then it was my turn.

"Thou shalt not steal. This is a commandment with countless meanings." I heard myself begin in the offhand casual conversational tone I had heard my father use to open his sermons from time immemorial. "What real meaning lies behind these words?"

Now slowly, gradually, I began building toward a crescendo the way my father always did in his sermons. I gathered more intensity. I introduced the crimes of Hitler. Soon I was shouting but not too loudly, yet I must reserve my thunder the way my father always did.

"Of all the things the Nazis had stolen, THEY HAVE DONE MORE," I said in a hoarse whisper, my father's most effective rhetorical device. "They have robbed cities and schools and homes. THEY HAVE DONE MORE," a hoarse whisper rapping the pulpit smartly for emphasis the way my father always did. "They have robbed libraries of their books and museums of their paintings. THEY HAVE DONE MORE," I hoarsely hammered the table harder. And now I was shouting—hoarsely, grandly, triumphantly, rabbinically. "THEY HAVE ROBBED THE GERMAN PEOPLE OF THEIR HERITAGE…" a significant pause like my father "AND THEIR FREEDOM."

I stopped abruptly. I was done. I listened. A hush, yes a deep utter hush, had fallen over the congregation. So I thought this is what it was like to shout from a pulpit to stir a congregation. In a triumphant swish of marquisette I spun around and returned to my seat.

The hush was real enough. But it was my mimicry, so perilously close to caricature, that had struck the congregation dumb—not my eloquence and certainly not my message which was hardly news in 1943. I did not see it that way however. Snuggling proudly back in my chair and making way for Rita Doctofsky on Coveting, I felt I had struck a mighty blow for freedom.

I was 15 when the war ended. One day shortly thereafter my English teacher hailed me in the hall of the high school and asked me if I would like to be on a radio program where teenagers would discuss "Can the United Nations Keep the Peace?"

"The what?"

"The United Nations.

"Oh."

I recalled dimly having heard the word mentioned once while flicking the radio dial from Blind Date to Easy Aces. I thought for a moment.

"Gosh yes, I'd love to be on the radio."

The program was produced by an enthusiastic little woman who believed fervently in "out of the mouths of babes" and who hung on avidly to our every word but who nonetheless protected herself and us by providing handy little scripts reminding us what we thought.

I was lined up on the Affirmative side arguing "Yes, the United Nations could keep the peace." On the Negative side however was a handsome dynamic boy from New York (I was just becoming susceptible to such influences) who argued what the postwar world really needed was a World Government.

I was instantly converted to World Government and returned home to form a chapter of World Federalists at our school. Zealously we spread the word. We sent letters to editors. We published a paper. We passed out leaflets on the street corners.

As you may have heard, no world government was formed. However we did command the interest and attention of many worthy citizens who suspected that our very age endowed us with some special insight into things.

"Remember, Bertha," I heard one such man remark to his wife. "These kids have known nothing but the horrors of war since they were ten years old."

"Depression babies too," sniffed Bertha respectfully.

# 5

# Saturday Walk

When I was a little girl in Perth Amboy, New Jersey the "Saturday Walk" was an institution, a special weekly ritual shared by my father and me. Saturday was "shabbos," our day of rest, but it did not really begin for my father until noon, when he returned from his morning at the Temple. And *that*, he would give us to understand as he sighed and sat down to lunch, had not been restful at all, what with the difficulty of rounding up a minyan, the hassle with Klein the Shamus over how many chairs to set up for tomorrow's wedding, and the aggravation with the president of the Brotherhood who'd forgotten to remind members of Monday's meeting.

But that was all behind him now. Rising from lunch, he visibly shed the cares of the week as he called, "Judy, ready for our walk?" Of course I was. I had already assembled my five library books. He gathered up his eight, and we were off.

We walked very slowly; partly because he must adjust his grownup stride to my short-legged one; partly because he had "all the time in the world" today and wished to savor it. But we also walked slowly, I know, to allow my father to stop and "schmooze" with almost everyone we met.

Our walk had barely begun when, three houses down, I began to feel our pace slacken. Up on the porch, chattering like magpies, sat the Hungarians, an intimate enclave of Jews who had "brought each other over" from Hungary.

"Hello there! Good shabbos," called my father. "Mr. Fenyves, Mrs. Lichtman! How is your lumbago, Mr. Spitz?"

Instantly the babble ceased. The porch sat electrified. Every face lit up.

"Oy, it's Rabbi Davidson! Rabbi, won't you come up and have some fruit? Just for a minute?"

"Well, just for a minute." Actually, he didn't need any coaxing. A rocker was eagerly prepared for him. I too was fussed over and given a large piece of prune cake. I resigned myself to a game of hopscotch. Fifteen minutes later when I tuned in again, I was impressed but not the least bit surprised to discover my father holding the floor on Budapest. He had never been to Budapest (and they had grown up there), but he had some marvelous stories. The Hungarians were laughing and crying at once.

I was used to everyone looking up to my father, it was only natural. Still, I felt a small glow of pride. But they had monopolized him long enough. I tugged at his hand. Presently, he began to back down the steps, still schmoozing. Reluctantly, they let him go and we were on our way again.

A few doors down, Morris Filenbaum called from his porch.

"Rabbi! I've been meaning to tell you how much I enjoyed your sermon last Friday night; the one about courage."

Up the stairs we went. "It hit home," Mr Filenbaum continued. "I could use some courage right now. Business is very bad—everybody's using cloth handbags this season." Mr. Filenbaum manufactured leather handbags.

"Oh, is that so?" said my father. "Now why should that be? I would imagine leather would be much more durable." He listened, fascinated, as Mr Filenbaum explained the ins and outs of the handbag trade. In this manner, through various members of the congregation, my father had become something of an expert on the shoe, necktie, grocery, dry-cleaning, and frozen foods businesses.

He nudged me to remind me to thank Mr. Filenbaum for his latest handbag. As far back as I could remember, a new pocket-book from Mr. Filenbaum had always arrived just at the moment when the previous pocketbook was starting to fray. This miraculous timeliness I took for granted, like the pocketbooks themselves: they were my due, like the discount for shoes at Slobodiens. I managed a perfunctory thank-you-very-much.

"Nothing's too good for the rabbi's family!" Mr. Filenbaum exclaimed, beaming at me. They shmoozed a little longer, then we set off once more.

Passing the home of Jaffe the Tailor, we usually found Jaffe and his wife sitting side by side on their little porch. Behind them in their tailor shop the usual smell of irons was missing; Jaffe was the only member of the congregation I knew of who closed his business on shabbos (except us, of course, but we were special). I connected it with his great age and flowing beard, which struck me as Biblical or at least orthodox; but no, he belonged to our Conservative temple. He always insisted on altering our coats and hemming our skirts for nothing; it was a privilege, he said. Now, he buttonholed my father on a point of Talmudic law.

My father warmed to the subject, loving to tell how everything had changed through the years and how Rabbi Akiba had disagreed with Rabbi Ben-Eliezer. I left them to

35

browse through the little shop, playing with the cool irons and fingering the silent sewing machines. Finally they were finished, and we made our way up Madison Avenue.

Slowly, leisurely, lazily we ambled up the avenue nodding to people on porches, gazing in grocery windows, pausing to watch a softball game in an empty lot. I called the high school "my school," though I knew I couldn't go there for years and years. Whenever we reached the large rambling vine-covered building, I insisted on running about its empty grounds and hopping from stone to stone along its wall, while my father waited below with an indulgent smile upon his face.

"Look, daddy, this is *my* school: I'm the only one here!"

"So I see."

"Will I go here someday?"

"Yes, when you're much bigger."

"And will I like my school?"

"Of course." There was not a trace of doubt in his voice.

At Brody's Ice Cream Parlor we always stopped for a soda. Then my father chose a good cigar, to be pocketed and saved for after shabbos. Mr. Brody (one of those shadowy figures who "belonged to the other shul") smilingly entered it on our bill to be paid later, because it was understood by everyone that the rabbi didn't handle money on shabbos.

At the Five Corners we cut across Perth Amboy's main business thoroughfare, with its frantic Saturday commerce, and headed for Jefferson Street a block beyond, which seemed dignified and subdued with its row of official buildings. Past the YMCA we went, hailing Mr. Forest its executive director; past the Perth Amboy Evening News with a wave for Dave Merman, the city editor (an agnostic Jew for whom my father had a grudging respect); up the steps of the post office to open up the Temple's box; and finally, the climax, the high point of our afternoon—across the street to the public library!

This was no casual visit but a serious, all-afternoon undertaking. First we would sit for a couple of hours by the magazine rack, browsing through the latest issues of all the journals, lay and scholarly: my father believed in "being up on things." Then came a careful perusal of the new books: he had reservations on several. He read everything (poetry, history, biography), but his secret vice was the mysteries, which he devoured. While he browsed, I slipped into the children's room and made a leisurely selection. It was quiet, comfortable, leisurely in the library, everyone whispering or reading at tables. It was the place that shabbos most was.

Finally my father would come around to pick me up in the children's room. Our arms full of books, we started off. As soon as we had left, he became engrossed in "The Sunburnt Corpse." It was my responsibility to shepherd him across streets as he read. We talked little, but there was peace in the air between us as we walked along. Sometimes a passing car would pull up and a voice—possibly that of Irving Pearlstein, chairman of Temple Seats—would call, "Can I give you a lift somewhere, Rabbi?"

"No, thanks. It's shabbos…we walk today!" he replied gaily.

"Oops! I forgot!" A little embarrassed, Irving would drive off.

If the day was fair, on the way home we stopped at the municipal tennis courts along the river. There was Hetz Levine hitting the ball to skinny old Ted Ernest, who always sucked a cherry-pit while he played. "Rabbi Davidson, hello!" cried big, florid Bill Rhodes, who ran the courts for the city. "Have a seat!" It was understood that my father, who was a local doubles champion, didn't play tennis on shabbos.

"Rab, have you noticed the improvement in Ted's service?" called Benny Baron, the small, swarthy tennis pro, shuffling out to greet us.

Sitting in the sun between Benny and Bill, commenting on the play, my father was obviously enjoying himself, the taxing round of weddings, funerals, temperamental choirs, and bickering organizations temporarily set aside for Saturday afternoon. I felt good, too, as I skipped about the lawns and shimmied up the wire fence that ran around the courts.

But finally we rose to go. It was past four; we had been gone since one. When we arrived home, my parents would lie down for their Saturday afternoon nap, and I would run outside to play jump-rope with my friends, who had been awaiting my return.

---

A SENSE OF PRIVILEGE INFORMED THESE SATURDAY afternoons of my childhood. That everyone knew us, that we did not pay for our sodas in quite the same manner as others did, all this gave me a feeling of being special, luckier than others. My security was total. And these Saturday afternoons were times of lazy joy. Between that time and the later time of adolescence was an interim period when I did not feel deprived or excluded on shabbos, but only a little uncomfortable, vaguely different. No head-on collision between my desires and the shabbos had yet occurred; the hobbling, inhibiting side of shabbos did not yet loom large; still, there was just enough of it to make me feel a bit uncomfortable on shabbos afternoon.

We were ten pre-teens, a close-knit set of Jewish girls from the better side of town, the tonier congregation, inseparables from morning to night, and Saturday afternoon was movie afternoon. We walked to the movies as a group, ten strong, sitting in a line in a certain row with a scramble to decide who sat next to whom; and all the phoning beforehand to determine who was going, and what we would wear.

I was permitted to go with the rest. Whatever factors prompted my father to acquiesce in this somewhat unshabbos-like activity, I shall never know. I do not recall my going ever being an issue; the girls went to the movies Saturday and I went with them. At some point along the way the "Saturday Walk" had become a thing of the past.

Of course, I could not spend money to enter, that went without saying. I had a pass from the Ditmas Theatre, a clerical courtesy card which admitted "One Plus A Friend." One week I admitted Janice, the next week Elaine, the following week Barbara; and this gave me a certain social leverage. But I can remember blushing and feeling conspicuous when I presented my courtesy card after the others had paid their way, and I remember feeling embarrassed when I had to ask my playmates to buy popcorn or candy for me.

A vague embarrassment at being different was gnawing at me but was not yet big enough to hurt. And a Clark Gable movie, while perhaps not so joyous as the old Saturday Walks, was certainly diverting. The group of ten girls remained cohesive, and as we entered adolescence there began to accrue to it all the tyrannical conformism of the teenage set.

One day I found myself in high school; it was a new world, and this world revolved around the Saturday afternoon football game. Yes, there were classes and we all managed to get good grades, for we were all bound for college. And yes, there was the Latin Club, and the School Paper, and other activities. But they fooled no one. The thing that really counted was the football game; the girls that really counted were the cheerleaders; the boys that really counted were the football team. Here was glory and romance, here was social status, and the most important day of the week was, of course, Saturday.

> *"Ee Aye Dombrowski!*
> *Yay, yay Dombrowski!*
> *He's a man*
> *Who's a man?*
> *He's an Amboy High School man:*
> *Ee Aye Dombrowski!"*

As I heard this cheer, ringing passionately through the crisp, cold fall air, my heart began to pound, and then to ache. And the music, the militant chants of conquest:

> *"The Amboy line*
> *Goes marching on*
> *Down the field, in the quest of the fray*
> *The Amboy song*
> *Goes ringing on*
> *Its melody resounding*
> *Ever and aye*
> *So come and join the throng*
> *That help along*
> *The fighting Panthers that wear our colors so gay*
> *As we ever*
> *Yes ever*
> *By mighty*

*Endeavor*
*Fight on to Victory, the Amboy way!"*

*"T-E-A-M*
*Yaaaaaaaaaay, Team!*
*T-E-A-M*
*Yaaaaaaaaaay, Team!*
*T-E-A-M*
*Yaaaaaaaaaay, Team!*
*TEAM, TEAM, TEAM!"*

It was war, and marching, and heraldry. It was all the color, romance, and vigor of war and combat. It was patriotism, and we were moved by it. So strong was our young feeling for the red and white that once, when Camille Ratajak was slapped by a Woodbridge policeman after the hard-fought Thanksgiving Game with Woodbridge, the whole school, led by a militant rabble-rouser named Frank Finno, rode in a great honking caravan of cars all the way to Woodbridge for redress (it was a Thursday, so I went too).

The heroes of the school were big, muscular, handsome blond Poles and Ukrainians…Dombrowski, Paledewich, Gronsky, thus rang the roster of our Catalog of Heroes, the football program. It was their courage and heroism we watched with reverence as they smashed through the scrimmage line to victory; as they fell on the field of battle and had to have their noses plugged by the medical squad (run by a Jewish boy). It was they who were pulled out of the game, and were suddenly sent back in to save the day for Amboy High, and how we howled when they dashed onto the field at the last minute and plunged through the line for a touchdown. This was what life was all about. And the cheerleaders, chosen for their beautiful blond hair and their grace, as well as their skill and the power of their lungs, they were part of it all. They were the home front, the first line of patriotism.

"C'mon, the team yell, the team yell!" they exhorted us through their beautiful red and white megaphones, and we responded, shouting ourselves hoarse for Dombrowski, for Gronsky, for Amboy.

At first the "Big ten," our group of ten Jewish girls, had treated it all with a certain amount of reserve and snobbery. Nothing in their background had quite prepared them for this kind of patriotic fervor: their grandfathers had been hunted down by the authorities in Minsk, had smuggled sugar from Kiev to Moscow in the hems of their pants, and deserted the Polish Army. Moreover, it was told that our heroes didn't study, got mediocre grades, said "ain it?" and had even in private been heard to utter rather anti-Semitic remarks. For a while our patriotism was faint-hearted.

But all the force of our age and our school was working upon us; moreover, Dombrowski and Gronsky were handsome and virile ("our" boys, dark and skinny, seemed rather pale beside them). We were on the brink, and needed only a style-setter to push us overboard.

Elaine was our style-setter. At first withholding her endorsement, by the end of the freshman year Elaine herself was calling Dombrowski on the telephone, saying "guess who," and soon we had all embraced the spirit of the school. Ten of us would gather in Elaine's living room, and, when her mother had left, would call up one of the football players and worshipfully talk for hours. Once we took a bike-hike to Gronsky's, way on the other side of town, to present him with a box of candy. Then, when tryouts for the cheerleaders came, we all practiced hard; I stood in front of my mirror for hours on end rehearsing the motions—though, of course, I was not able to try out, for cheerleaders had to ride on Saturdays.

By the time the fall of sophomore year rolled round, we had actually placed one of our own girls on the cheering squad; we all had red "beanies," red skirts, close-knit white turtle-neck sweaters, and a little lapel pin shaped like a panther which we wore directly over our hearts. This was the accepted costume for the football game and woe to her who departed from it. But while I wore my beanie as gallantly as the rest, I found myself becoming an outcast—more and more with every passing week. For everybody, *everybody* rode the bus to the football game, which was held at the stadium on the outskirts of town.

The bus trip was more than a means of getting to the game. It was a vital part of the whole ritual which culminated in victory or defeat and the bus trip homeward. Important things happened on that bus. Songs were sung. Cheers were cheered. Arrangements were made for obtaining players' autographs during the intermission. In short, if there was one place a person had to be, it was seated on that bus Saturday afternoon, going to the game.

Of course, riding on shabbos was unthinkable—I don't believe the possibility ever crossed my mind. But to miss the game was also unthinkable. So every week I walked the six miles to the game, alone. And slowly, inexorably, I became an outcast.

In the beginning, it was sometimes possible to find a friend to accompany me, since I had a rabbinical courtesy card "Admitting Two." But soon even this lure became powerless. It was simply too much of a sacrifice to ask of anyone; it was just too important to be on that bus.

So I walked to the game alone, and when I arrived I sat alone, as it was impossible to find or, if finding, to reach any group in those wildly pressing throngs. And though I howled more loudly than anyone; and though the tears came when I sang "To Thee, the School I Love So Well"; And though my white wool socks were turned down just right and my panther pin lay just above my heart; and though I yelled for Dombrowski, passionately, and hissed the Visitors—all the while I knew that somewhere up in the stands sat the crowd, giggling and conspiring together. And during intermission as I sipped my solitary orange drink I knew that somewhere the gang, in a fever of excitement, was stealing over to the shower-rooms to await Dombrowski and get his autograph. And after the game, as I walked home alone along the edges of cemeteries, it was a long painful trek seeming more like sixteen miles than six, the silence punctured by the whirling by of gaily bedecked autos driven by seniors and plastered with huge red and white stickers saying Crush Cartaret, with swarms of students leaning out the windows shouting school songs; and sometimes the bus—*The* Bus, itself—suddenly streaked past with a great burst of noise and laughter, depositing snatches of cheers on the raw November air.

I would huddle up into my turtleneck, head bent, wishing I were invisible, wishing I were dead, feeling completely left out, different, "square" (me, the special one!)

This feeling of being "square" grew more and more intense as our crowd became friendlier with football players and cheerleaders. (They got particularly chummy at Away Games. Not everyone went to Away Games, but our girls, now the most ardent camp followers in the school, never missed one. And as for me, I would have walked the fifty miles to Newark gladly had it been physically possible.) Elaine and Gronsky exchanged wisecracks in the halls; a majorette named Doris Karee taught Rita fancy twirling; and the girls began to accumulate a store of Saturday afternoon anecdotes and reminiscences of which I knew nothing. All week long they kept exchanging notes about Saturday—what had happened last Saturday, what they would do next Saturday, some intrigue, some cryptic word uttered by Otlowski during intermission that must be deciphered, what someone had said to so-and-so on the Bus.

And one day in French class a note was passed across me (across me!) from May to Janice, which I, by sheer force of habit, started to open.

"Oh, it's not for you, Judy. It's about Saturday."

Oh, naturally! Not for me, about Saturday! Between classes I stopped in the ladies' room and wept bitterly.

One day, my heart cringing at the prospect of another long lonely walk to the game, I called my friend Donna, hoping against hope that she would walk with me. But no, she was awfully sorry but she was meeting the kids at the bus stop in three minutes.

Evidently my father, who had just arrived home from the Temple (irritated because Klein the Shamus had misspelled a name on the Memorial Tablet) felt sorry for me because he said, "Say, I wouldn't mind taking in the game today—why don't we walk there together?"

Years of Saturday movies separated this time from the Saturday Walks of childhood. I think we both felt a pang of sentiment. "Okay," I said, and a minute later bit my tongue, assailed by a sense of foreboding. But it was too late, he was already putting on his coat.

This was a really long walk that dwarfed the strolls of childhood. It was necessary to walk fast if we were to make it by two thirty. My mother, beaming, waved us off. I wore my costume of white wool socks, red skirt, white turtleneck sweater; he wore his invariable rabbinical black—black pants, black coat, navy blue tie, a tan vest underneath to keep him warm. We sped past Brody's, past the Y, the post office, the library—why, I wondered, did he have to wear such conservative colors? Everyone else at the game would wear sports jackets and a dash of color like a red scarf.

But he appeared oblivious to my mounting apprehension. Though we were pressed for time he managed to stop for a short schmooze with Tex Rosen. Always a gadget lover, he had brought along a pair of field glasses which hung around his neck like an albatross, giving him, I thought, an outlandish look. The first few miles were not so bad, but as we approached the vicinity of the stadium, and the game began to make itself felt, my uneasiness assumed great proportions. Boisterous buses rolled past, full of screaming classmates. Fragments of the band, dressed in red pants and white blouses, trying out tubas and trumpets, rushed by. What on earth was I doing here with my father, for God's sake? It was all wrong, the ultimate *faux pas*. Finally, with a great whoop the important bus bearing the team sped past, and my mortification was complete: the team had seen me going to the game with my father.

At the gate I drew a deep breath and plunged in. Inside, it was even worse than I had feared. My father and I had to pick our way through arm-linked, banner-waving groups of students swaying in unison. I hurried him over to an inconspicuous spot near the Ten Yard Line where, I hoped, nobody would see us.

The game was already in progress. I hunched up in my sweater and watched glumly. Beside me my father appeared to be enjoying himself to the hilt. Squinting through his field-glasses, he kept his eye on the ball and always seemed to know where it was. Evidently he had read the Perth Amboy Evening News the night before because he knew who played what and how good they were. He was also, it turned out, an expert on the intricacies of scoring and tried to explain to me the difference between a field goal and a safety goal. But I was barely listening. I was just praying for the game to be over so that I could hurry him home.

Amboy High won an unprecedented, smashing victory, 76 to 6. As we left the stadium I noticed something unusual; rather than running for the buses as was customary, the students were all lining up in the street behind the band. Then I caught on: once in a great while (twice since I'd been in school), to celebrate a really great victory, the bus ride was canceled and everyone marched home through the streets— a great throng charging through the streets of Perth Amboy shouting our cheers and songs until, at the Five Corners, all traffic stopped while the twirlers performed in a great feverish victory celebration.

"You march home with them, I have a couple of stops to make anyway," smiled my father. I nodded and he left.

Lines were forming in the street, martial row upon martial row; the majorettes were starting to lift their feet in compelling rhythms, the band was tuning up, the cheerleaders were whipping up enthusiasm.

> "*T-E-A-M*
> *Yaaaaaaaaaaaaaaaay, Team!*

T-E-A-M
*Yaaaaaaaaaaaaaaaay, Team!"*

Just then I spotted my crowd marching past, arms linked, goose-stepping more handsomely than anyone else, waving their programs just signed by today's punting heroes. Seeing me, they waved and beckoned me to join them, and Janice at the end of the row proffered an arm. I should have been overjoyed. With one step I could be one with the marching mob. "No, I don't feel like it," I heard myself calling.

And suddenly it all appalled and repelled me, the rows of marchers, the blaring trumpets, the rhythmic chanting cheers; and in our wild pursuit of Dombrowski I thought I saw something slavish. "Who wants it?" I thought. I didn't. For the first time in many months I straightened up and lifted my head high; an old assurance crept back into my voice. I took my own route home, and this time the autumn air seemed bracing and the way did not feel very long at all.

The following week I walked to the game in a green plaid skirt and yellow cardigan. Sometimes I went to the games, sometimes I didn't. I started reading proof for the school paper and joined a square-dancing group. Never again would I follow a mob or yell for a team.

And what of shabbos, you ask? Oh yes, shabbos. It became increasingly inconvenient, until three years later I rejected it altogether, for what I was sure were purely philosophical reasons.

# 6

# My Father and Religion

When I was a teenager—probing, questioning, doubting—a monster my father himself had created by encouraging me to read, I constantly tortured him with questions. Did he really believe in God? What was God like? Was there life after death?

He always wriggled out of answering such questions, retreating behind the *New York Times* or a mystery novel, implying that such things could not be answered directly and should remain implicit. At the time I thought him a hypocrite. He was, after all, a well-known rabbi, an eloquent preacher and a Sunday school teacher. He should have clear cut answers to my questions about God or else he should quit his job.

I know now he could not answer them because I think the thing that drew him to Judaism was the poetry. I think the poetry was the real thing for him.

My father wrote three poems. He wrote his own wedding song, dedicated to my mother, called "Take Thou my Vow," a romantic song in which he and my mother would fly on whispering wings. He wrote the Sunday school song of Temple Beth Morgan called "Come Rise Ye My People and Sing of Our Temple," a rather sing-songy, goody goody, rah

rah song quite beneath him, to the tune of "Marchita" and he also wrote the ritual of the order of the golden chain for a women's Masonic Lodge. I have never seen it, but believe it was full of romantic mysteries and cadences.

But his feeling for poetry was revealed by the poems he read to me at bedtime when I was a child.

It was not limericks, or funny poems, or even "Winken, Blinken, and Nod" that he read to me. When he came in, clenching his cigar in his teeth, and with the *Oxford Book of English Verse,* he read me the poetry of his heart—"Annabelle Lee," "The Bells," "The Raven," and most significantly, "Little Boy Blue."

They were all beautiful haunting melodic poems that haunt me still. But more interesting, of all things for a grown man to read to an impressionable little girl, they were all morbid tragic poems of death and lost loves and disappointments, such as Edgar Allen Poe's "Annabelle Lee":

> *It was many and many a year ago,*
> *In a kingdom by the sea,*
> *That a maiden there lived whom you may know*
> *By the name of Annabel Lee;*
> *And this maiden she lived with no other thought*
> *Than to love and be loved by me.*
>
> *I was a child and she was a child,*
> *In this kingdom by the sea,*
> *But we loved with a love that was more than love—*
> *I and my Annabel Lee—*
> *With a love that the wingèd seraphs of Heaven*
> *Coveted her and me....*

*The angels, not half so happy in Heaven,*
*Went envying her and me—*
*Yes!—that was the reason (as all men know,*
*In this kingdom by the sea)*
*That the wind came out of the cloud by night,*
*Chilling and killing my Annabel Lee.*

Also tragic, morbid, and haunted by death is the beautiful "Little Boy Blue" (by Eugene Fields) which he never tired of reading aloud to me, nor did I tire of hearing it. It was about a little boy Blue who loved his little toy dog and his little tin soldier, who were devoted to him also, but one day Little Boy Blue went to sleep and never woke up.

*The little toy dog is covered with dust,*
*But sturdy and stanch he stands;*
*And the little toy soldier is red with rust,*
*And his musket molds in his hands.*
*Time was when the little toy dog was new*
*And the soldier was passing fair,*
*And that was the time when our Little Boy Blue*
*Kissed them and put them there.*

*"Now, don't you go till I come," he said,*
*"And don't you make any noise!"*
*So toddling off to his trundle-bed*
*He dreamed of the pretty toys.*

*And as he was dreaming, an angel song*
*Awakened our Little Boy Blue,—*
*Oh, the years are many, the years are long,*
*But the little toy friends are true.*

Or "The Raven" with its sad, sad refrain "Nevermore, nevermore" will he see his lost Lenore.

Morbid, tragic, beautiful, what poetry for a grown man to read a little girl, especially a rabbi. Yet going to Friday night services week after week, with my hand in my mother's, to our synagogue where my father stood upon the podium in a black gown and read aloud the prayers, there was little apparent contradiction. For here again, to the enthralled ears of a child, was poetry of a different kind and read intoned by the same voice, my father's.

On Friday night, the great temple alight, the great room, the immensity of the high ceilings, the rabbi and cantor on the podium in their long gowns, the fresh flowers donated by Les Kaufman in a basket and lit candelabra, the invisible choir singing overhead, the small close-knit set of families, the faithful ones who came every Friday, my mother pretty and perfumed in white gloves nodding hello to the congregation despite her painful shyness, the air of a special day, the dramatic pause before the service began, and then my father moving toward the podium and his melodic voice carried by the echoes of the room:

> *LIFT UP YE HEADS OH YE GATES*
> *AND MAY YE LIFT THEM UP*
> *YE EVERLASTING DOORS THAT*
> *THE KING OF GLORY MAY COME IN.*
> *WHO IS THE KING OF GLORY?*
> *THE LORD OF HOSTS,*
> *THE LORD MIGHTY IN BATTLE,*
> *HE IS THE KING OF GLORY.*
> *SELAH.*

Selah. The prayers were punctuated by the mysterious beautiful word. Selah. I had no idea what it meant but it made the prayers all the more wonderful.

And the wonderful prayer introducing the Sabbath, comparing the Sabbath with a bride: "Come my dear to meet the Bride…"

And prayers about God creating the world:

*He stretched forth the heavens and laid the foundations of the earth. His glory is revealed in the heavens above and His might is manifest in the loftiest heights. He is our God, there is none other. In truth he is our King, there is none besides him. Thus it is written in his Torah: Know this day and consider it in thy heart that the lord He is God in the heavens above and on the earth beneath there is none else.*

And on the High Holy Days, the great room now crammed with people and an air of holiness and expectancy. My heart burst when my father, now in his white robe for the High Holy Days, would come to the special part of the service that I most loved—in fact waited for all year long.

*On New Year's Day the decree is inscribed, and on the Day of Judgment it is sealed—Who shall live and who shall die? Who shall and who shall not reach the limit of man's days? Who shall perish by fire and who by water? Who by sword and who by shield? Who by hunger and who by thirst? Who shall have peace and who shall wander?*

Beautiful poetry and fatalistic. But then, corrected for in the next paragraph, pure prose and clearly, to a child's mind, an afterthought:

> *But penitence, prayer, and charity avert the evil decree.*

Throughout my childhood these beautiful cadences of the religious services intoned in my father's voice, wholly sensitive to their rhythms and read with intense feeling and with a great sense of their rhythms and cadences—amazing since he was tone deaf to music—reverberated through my consciousness, superimposed on all the morbid, beautiful poetry of the earlier years.

I think now it was the aspect of the religion which my father loved too. But the poetry of the service was affirmative, the poetry he loved to read to us as children was not affirmative—it was morbid and it spoke of death, destruction, and disappointment.

I think now that it was the earlier poetry that more accurately reflected my father's lifelong attitude—pessimism and melancholy. I was never able to get him to discuss an afterlife.

Religion did not sustain him in his final agony and I suspect he saw death as final.

When my father died, his leg consumed by gangrene, they buried him in his white Rosh Hashanah robes. What would he finally have thought if he saw himself lying in his grave? I think he would have been more impressed by the reality of the rot than of the reality of the rabbinical robe.

# 7

# Mama

"People are like horses," my grandmother used to say when she pared our nails. "There are the strong —horses built to carry heavy loads— they're short and thick and ugly; then there are the beautiful, graceful race horses and show horses, who have to be pampered and cared for." My grandmother, whom we called Mama, whispered these words to me once in the middle of the night. She always slept in my room when she came for an overnight visit, and our midnight conversations were a great joy to us both. This particular remark, I recall, was for some reason distasteful to me, but I shrugged it off. My beautiful, graceful grandmother, with the long lustrous grey hair, light-hearted, light-headed—how could one possibly quarrel with her? It was only years later, in a darker hour, that the remark came back to me, and I felt for my grandmother a sudden shiver of apprehension.

Mama's early years are buried in shadow, but there is just a suggestion of cloistered, sheltered schoolyard, clean shining waxed floors, and charming white pantaloons. A sheltered girlhood led easily into the shelter of a loving, happy marriage: Mama's good fortune was firmly grounded in the fact that she had found exactly the right man at the age of eighteen. She and Pa had eloped on the way to the Army-Navy Thanksgiving game while he was a student at dental school; ever afterward the anniversary was celebrated as part of the Thanksgiving feast, with Mama and Pa holding hands and exchanging loving glances over the turkey. Pa was a loving and protective husband; he insisted that Mama have help with the housework and plenty of help with their three daughters. She was not to trouble herself with money matters and other trying masculine business-—Mama never went to the bank and never learned to write a check. She had charge accounts at Bamberger's that covered her needs while out shopping (her favorite pastime). Of her, he expected the loving care of the family, and her love bubbled over and enveloped us all. Of course, she was not expected to be exacting in her household duties; often it was that Mama, carried away by a thrilling tour of Woolworth's and a stop at Schrafft's, would appear at home at six having forgotten to prepare anything for supper. The family just laughed and played the phonograph while Mama got busy in the kitchen. Even the family dog, Skippy, was indulgent. When Pa bought Skippy he explained to Mama that he would take care of the dog, bathe him, brush him, take him for walks, and that is exactly what he did. Mama shouldn't have to bother herself with a dirty, sheddy old dog.

A visit from Mama (she and Pa lived in Newark, thirty miles away) was always a special treat because she hugged us a lot and laughed a lot, sitting over cups of coffee with my mother. The biggest treat of all was a walk downtown, where we always wound up in Woolworth's. Mama loved to browse among the dazzling trinkets, and invariably emerged with a pretty potholder for Fanny, a hairnet for my mother, and a new type of bath-salt for Rose. "I stayed in bed Sunday until

12 o'clock," she would write Rose, sending along the bath-salt. "Then I jumped in the tub with Bath-A-Sweet, it's great. Be sure to try your soap." The best thing about these walks was that Mama's sunshine poured upon total strangers. She was always complimenting a fireman on his splendid dog, or stopping a salesgirl to ask what she used on her face to make it so rosy. Eagerly, the girl would reveal her beauty secret, with Mama nodding and exclaiming, and the two would part old friends. When she stayed overnight it was always an amazement to me when she combed out her hair before bed, it was so much longer than one realized during the day, almost the hair of an innocent young girl. It came down to her waist, and was so thick and lustrous as she brushed it. I thought her very beautiful, and not like a grandmother at all, though I knew she must be old (maybe 50, even) and her hair was iron grey, she seemed like a young girl. And when she turned out the light and started giggling over this and that, she seemed even more like a young girl. It was lack of care that kept her young—I knew this in my young bones, though I could not have explained it to anybody. Only sometimes, in the middle of the night, the family in the apartment above would make a noise, and it used to surprise me how upset Mama would get, "Oh! Oh! They must be moving furniture! Oh, why don't they stop?" she would groan. And she would get a splitting headache and I would have to massage her scalp until she felt better. At home, she told me, when she got one of her headaches Pa would massage her scalp. He was such a dear, such a darling. Then she'd start getting homesick for Pa, and usually the next day, to our disappointment, she would depart for home.

Mama saw Pa as the most remarkable of men, and indeed he had become a successful and popular figure in

Newark. Like an infatuated schoolgirl, she clipped from the paper any notice of his achievements—as dental surgeon, organizer of clinics, president of Kiwanis— and compiled large scrapbooks of his deeds, which, however, she showed only to her daughters, being too modest to display them to others. Although she rarely visited his office (the neighborhood was changing, Pa said; an unpleasant dirty street, a dusty bus ride, why should Mama have to go there?), she followed his career proudly, and knew him as a dental surgeon of unequalled prowess.

Once a week, once they were married, Fanny, Lillian and Rose would meet Mama at Bamberger's and spend a delightful day browsing. They didn't buy much, they were not spendthrifts; it was just the sport of shopping they enjoyed. In late afternoon, amid gales of laughter, they would wind up at the Dutch Tea Room for cream cheese and olive sandwiches and coffee, and they all bloomed, especially Mama.

Then one September day, when I was fourteen, the phone rang at 6 am. My mother answered. "Oh my God," she cried, "Max, come quick, something awful has happened to Pa!" My father came running, "What is it?" "He was mugged: "He was walking the dog and he was mugged!" My father grabbed the phone. When he hung up, his face was ashen. He took my mother aside and they talked quietly. Later, they told us, Pa had gone out last night, as usual, to walk Skippy. Three teenage boys jumped on him, hit him on the head with a flashlight, and stole his wallet. Someone found him and carried him up to the apartment. When Mama opened the door, they carried him in and lay him on the couch. Mama had thought he was dead. Pa came to, finally, but he was very bad, the doctor couldn't tell how bad.

Pa stayed in the hospital for a month. A silent, stunned Mama sat by his side all the time, Finally, he was pronounced well enough to go home. But he was not himself. He was weak and shaky, grown old overnight, his memory fuzzy. At home, Mama waited on him hand and foot, fetched and carried, walked the dog. She tried to be cheerful to keep up Pa's spirits, but we could see the effort it took. When they went out Mama helped him down the stairs and into a cab.

To everyone's surprise, Pa had saved very little money. He insisted on resuming his dental practice as soon as he could stand on his feet. It turned out that he was still able to perform the more routine jobs, like drilling and filling; but the dental surgery was too much for him, his fingers not steady enough. Since his practice was shrinking, and nearly all of his savings had been drained off by hospital bills, he could no longer afford an office nurse, and Mama had to fill in. It shocked me the first time I saw her in a starched white uniform, her arm linked in Pa's. She would rise every morning at seven and walk down the stairs with him. It must never appear that she thought he needed help on the stairs. Pa was very touchy about any helplessness or dependence on Mama. He would lean on her lightly as they climbed the flight of stairs to the dental office. Once there, she would wipe off the instruments as he prepared for patients. Slowly he taught her the rudiments of the dental assistant's job: names of instruments, names of compounds she must hand him. At five, they closed the office and went home; Mama would help him up the stairs, then fix the supper and walk the dog.

So it went from winter into early spring. Pa insisted on remaining in charge of family finances, writing checks in his wobbly hand; but it was Mama who must fend off the creditors who now began to hound them, "Why hello, Mr. Thomas" I heard her saying into the phone, one April day when I dropped by the office, "A bill? What bill are you speaking of?" (She was all feigned innocence; Mama dissembling?) "Ohh yes, now I remember. Why, I guess it just slipped our mind this month, Mr, Thomas. Two months? Really? Time does fly, doesn't it? Uh... could you just wait two more weeks, Mr. Thomas? Why, how dare you speak that way to me, after all the years you and Pa played bridge at the Progress Club... I don't..." A patient had entered the office, and Mama quickly placed her hand over the receiver, a furtive gesture so unlike her I saw that her fingers were trembling: "Hello, Mrs. Harris," she said with forced cordiality. Her face was veiled and guarded, so different from her old, friendly, outgoing face. "Won't you sit down please, the doctor will be with you in just a moment." "Hey Jenny, give me a hand with this x-ray." called Pa. "Coming," mama called. A man emerged from the inner rooms, muttering angrily. Mama was running after him trying to placate him. "Oh Mr. Haynes, the doctor has never done that before! It must have slipped. It will never happen again... just bathe it in ice water." "I'll never come here again, that's for sure," the man declared, and slammed the door.

The office was empty and quiet, now. Mama sighed, sank into a hard plastic chair, and rubbed her head. She loosened the hairpins, and all the soft, grey hair tumbled down over her shoulders. It pained me to see that it was thick and grey and lustrous still, the mane of a filly. "Mama, what was it you told me that time when I was a little girl, about people being like horses, some built to carry heavy loads... how did it go again?" She stared at me blankly and shook her head, she never smiled at us anymore, and never hugged us. All of the warmth and affection had gone out of her. But suddenly, I recalled the saying; and I shuddered with dread for Mama.

When one of Pa's checks bounced, it was discovered that he had been carrying several checks for deposit around in his pocket for weeks; and it became necessary for Mama to assume responsibility for writing and depositing checks. A man at the bank explained to her how it was done; she listened, straining attentively to grasp it all. But the bank, with its cold marble lobbies and poker-faced tellers, terrified and intimidated her. Every Friday at noon she took a bus to the bank, made out a deposit slip, and stood, white and rigid, in line to deposit the week's receipts.

Then one day, as Mama was rolling cotton balls for Pa, she began to scream. She screamed and screamed, people came running in from the street. Still she screamed. At length a car arrived and carried her off. But she continued to scream. At the mental hospital (where she was thereafter confined), it took them three days to stop that screaming.

# 8

# Yule Log

Christmas was always a time of tension. At school we would feel the first tugs about the middle of October, when pupils were picked for the cast of the Christmas program, handmade gifts for mommy and daddy were planned, and a tree appeared in the corner of the classroom.

It was understood that I, the rabbi's daughter, did not appear in Christmas plays and I was never asked; but many of the children at P.S. Number 7 were Jewish and often the Christmas pageant was enacted by Dwight Halpern, Stanton Levy and Herman Cohen as the Three Wise Men.

There was little resistance to all this on our part. If we fashioned our ornaments and drew our trees a little half-heartedly, nobody noticed. There was, however, one point at which we offered passive resistance—the Christmas songs that were sung every day in assembly.

There had never been a conference where we plotted this resistance ; no Martin Luther King ever rallied us, we never even spoke of it to one another. It was simply something that had been done by Jewish children at Number 7 School from time immemorial: we would sing the carols with the rest, but whenever we came to a line with "Christ the Lord" in it we just moved our lips.

It confounds me that nobody ever spotted this…or did they? Did they ever notice that the resounding choruses of "Silent Night" suddenly became half audible when we reached the line "Christ the Savior is born"?

While we were solidly united in this practice, Santa Claus was another matter entirely. Santa Claus was the big problem, the borderline case, a matter of interpretation. Some of the Jewish children were great Santa Clausniks and my own Maplewood cousins, (to my father's chagrin), hung up their stockings on Christmas night. They called them Chanukah stockings though, my Aunt always assured my mother. My mother, as a matter of fact, couldn't have cared less, but my Aunt withered under my father's frown and sarcasm. The Santa Claus party contended that he was just a merry winter clown; the other party shot back that he was a Christian religious symbol to ensnare us, as a sort of Trojan horse —and that we should have no truck with him. My father was of this party and so, as his dutiful daughter, was I.

Christmas trees were another seduction. During the Christmas season my father would suggest that we take the long way home from Temple. This, he claimed, was a con-stitutional, a brisk cold weather stroll, but he didn't fool me a bit, it was really a tour of inspection. He was particularly critical on High Street, where most of the Temple's "big givers" lived—the backsliding of the rich was something he was always half-expecting

"Hah," he would remark, confirmed in his worst suspi-cions, "Kornfeld got a tree! Wouldn't you know! He might at least pull down his blinds!" A sigh of relief as we passed Levin's and found it all dim, but a howl of triumph at Birn-baum's: "How do you like that—Birnbaum with a Christmas tree, I never thought it of him," and so on. These people, if confronted, would explain that a tree is so pretty and does no harm—it's not religious, just seasonal. But my father would scoff. The pressures from the majority were too strong. We would be engulfed if not eternally vigilant. It was because the tree was so pretty that one must watch out especially for the children. Today a tree, tomorrow High Mass.

Christmas, then, one resisted because it conflicted with one's beliefs, it was a threat to our Judaism.

Therefore, when I got to college, I cast off my religion. It might have been expected then, that the problem of Christmas would have been exorcised.

I entered college kosher and left it agnostic. The change, however, was not so abrupt as it sounds—doubts had crept in long ago. And though I credited books and basement bull sessions, the roots of my revolt were really one part philosophical and three parts gastronomical. Those cans of kosher meatballs I warmed up every night on the small rusty hot plate in my college bedroom! They smelled up the entire dormitory, they were nauseating, I can smell them yet. They and similar inconveniences, figured far more than books in my religious turning.

Nevertheless, despite its earthy origins and whatever its original causes, my conversion was deep-seated and thorough-going. In the end it was not kosher meatballs and sabbath prohibitions I was discarding but—God. And while I did not make a lot of noise about it, I was quietly convinced and doggedly determined to follow my beliefs.

I was already a confirmed and deep-seated nonbeliever at the end of my junior year when I was awarded by the college the honor of being the Yule Log Bearer at the Christmas Ceremony.

This was a bolt out of the blue, a staggering honor. My grades had never been anything special. Now suddenly, in my junior year, I had gotten all As and stood highest in my class! (This was because, with Spanish and Algebra and Zoology finally out of the way I was now living on a steady, heady diet of "American Constitutional Principles," "The Idea of Freedom of Thought from Voltaire to Thomas Jefferson" and "The Last Days of the Weimar Republic.") At Christmas Ceremony every year the girl with the highest marks in each class carried the Yule Log in. It was an honor for which all with scholarly aspirations pined. I was thrilled and flattered and quite proud and pleased with myself. I pictured myself at the Christmas Ceremony—the big ceremony of the year at the white Dutch Reform college chapel—being honored under the eyes of gasping freshmen. There would be tall girls bearing candles, and wearing white dresses—the kind of hushed, dim, quasi-religious ceremony in which college fraternities and masonic groups revel.

Word got out fast that I was the Yule Log bearer. I was sitting reading in the college library that afternoon when a friend, Sybil, came up to me:

"Judy did I hear that you are going to carry the Yule Log?"

"Well as a matter of fact yes." I blushed modestly.

"Do you mean you are going to participate in the Christmas Ceremony?"

"Do you approve of a religious ceremony in a state college?"

---

SYBIL, LIKE ME, WAS AN AGNOSTIC. WHAT SHE DISAPPROVED of was a state institution putting any religious pressures on its students.

As a matter of fact, I had been too dazzled by the honor even to think of that. My first reaction was that Sybil was just jealous and was trying to snatch the honor away from me. "Oh c'mon, now it's not a religious ceremony really, it's just a sort of college custom to honor class leaders. It just happens to be around Christmas time—of course I'm taking it," I muttered. I turned my head back to my book, dismissing her.

But I couldn't dismiss the thought. The question Sybil had raised seemed to crop up in everything I read. Hidden meanings lurked in every page. Later that day I read my history assignment. It was about the rise of Hitler in Germany.

It told of how Hitler was able to get power because there were too few people with the strength of character to resist politically what looked like a popular wave. Slowly, inexorably, the book showed Hitler snowed everyone under.

I kept trying to keep my mind on the homework but my conscience kept pricking me. At first I didn't know what about, but finally I began to see myself—too weak-willed and spineless to resist the popular custom.

I was just going along with something that I knew was wrong—too weak to resist! Or, too dazzled by the honor! Because of course, Sybil was right. Douglass College was financed in large part by the state of New Jersey. Though it still had a private board of trustees this was a vestige from the old days when it had been a private religious college. Nowadays it drew most of its funds from the state and even called itself "The State College of New Jersey." Now if this were a private college I told myself it would be different. They would have a right to impose any religious service or custom they wished, but as a public state-supported institution they had no right to impose religious doctrines on the students.

As a child of the Enlightenment, then as a political liberal (not as a Jew), I opposed the Christmas Ceremony. Because let's face it, I told myself now that my eyes were opened, it was a plainly religious ceremony. The Yule log was a deeply religious Christmas symbol. And despite all the watered-down masonic type hokum, there were also references aplenty to the nativity, etc. Yes, it was a religious ceremony and as a citizen opposed to the state's espousing any religion, in the name of liberalism, I opposed it. How could I participate? I would not!

My armor shining, I slammed my book shut and dashed right over to the office that had sent me the note informing me 1 was to be the yule log-bearer. The office was unaccountably in the gym building and the woman in charge was named Miss Hood.

"Miss Hood, I'm Judy Davidson."

"Oh yes Judy. Do sit down. Oh congratulations on the honor"

"Thank you." Now that I was here I did not know just how to explain my point. I suddenly realized it was a subtle point, an abstraction and Miss Hood had something to do with keeping the gym suits straight and was even at this moment tidying up a bunch of bowling clubs.

How could I explain this to her? She was waiting expectantly.

"Oh…Miss Hood…I…you know I was asked…you wrote me saying I was to carry the Yule Log."

"Yes, of course. You must be very proud. It's a real achievement."

"Well, I'm terribly sorry Miss Hood, and it's not that I don't appreciate your asking me very much, but I have decided to decline."

She looked up quizzically. I saw a cloud gathering on her face. It would, I knew, soon be a thunderstorm. I braced myself for her hostility, anger, and incomprehension.

"You see, well, it's a religious ceremony and I don't believe a state college ought to have religious ceremonies. I mean the college is financed by the state and the state should not impose in any form any religious...I believe it's not..."

She looked at me blankly for a moment. I awaited her outburst. But slowly a look of cordiality and understanding came to her face.

"Oh. Oh! I see....yes, of course, I understand, you're Jewish..."

Ignoring this, I pressed on.

"I believe it's not....it is not right that people who do not have, for example, the Christian beliefs, say for example Muslims, or Buddhists, or say Jews, for example, should be forced to take part even passively in a Christian ceremony in a college supported by state funds and taxes."

Her expression of cordiality grew.

"I see! Of course! You're Jewish! You don't like to be part of a ceremony that goes against your religion."

"Oh no no, that´s not it at all... I'm not Jewish...I mean... I'm Jewish, but I'm not at all religious, it's not a question of my being religious, it's just that in principle I don't believe the state should have..."

But she wasn't listening anymore. From cordiality her expression had turned into downright admiration.

"Now dear, that's alright. I understand. A religious Jew naturally wouldn't want to be in a Christian service. I always admire people who really believe in their religion. There are too few religious ones left, especially at college! Of course I understand...you're a Jew and it goes against your religion.

Think no more of it. I admire your religious zeal!" Awed and respectful, she bowed me out.

I gave up. It was clearly impossible to make her see that I was protesting not as a religious Jew but as a liberal. I did stay out of the Christmas Ceremony, but my resistance did nothing to alter the custom, which is carried on to this day. Still they carry the Yule Log down. I was an exception, not a reformer; one who wished to sit this one out, not one who wished to destroy a custom. My refusal was sympathetically accepted, not as a disciple of Thomas Jefferson, but as a rabbi's daughter.

# 9

# My Father and Money

When my father died an impecunious rabbi everyone was amazed to learn that he had left a substantial estate.

Well not everyone, for my sisters and I, embarrassed, kept it a secret. Only Mel Rubin, his lawyer who handled the estate and who was equally amazed, because my father in his final days had been terrified of the poorhouse, knew. Mel was a limited, rather dull-witted fellow who had grown rich with a condominium in Florida and one in the Bahamas by charging on estates and plenty for divorces. He had concentrated on those lucrative fields of law and thrived. My father knew this of Mel but also knew he was loyal and would administer the estate fairly. My father saw Mel straight. He never confused wealth with brains or virtue. Still the fact that my father, unbeknownst to anyone, had squirreled away over $200,000, cast a whole new light on my father and money.

Always I realized looking back over the years there had been ambivalence. My father saw through the rich. He'd seen too many fools in his congregation who had accumulated wealth and worthy, smart men who had not. And yet, and yet, he was impressed.

One of his most memorable sermons was called "We Can't Go Back to School Until We've Been to Sachs Fifth Avenue." Dripping with sarcasm, the sermon took its text from the wording of a full-page ad he had seen in the New York Times just before school opened, which coincided with Rosh Hashanah, and the speech was a Rosh Hashanah speech. It was this timely and contemporary idiom which gave my father's sermons their fame and kept even old Mrs. Aneckstein awake in the back pew. I remember the speech well because it reinforced all my anti-materialistic ideas learned at my father's knee and redoubled my sense of superiority at being at Rosh Hashanah service in my cousin Hilda's hand-me-down dress while Rosalie, Paula, and Joan were dressed in designer wool dresses with Peck and Peck labels. The gist of the speech was this: the Sachs ad, whose philosophy he delicately hinted, was shared by many members of the congregation reflected an idea which was antithetical to Judaism. It made the clothes important instead of knowledge, learning, study, and education. It was school that was important he explained, not what we wore to school or what the labels read. It was not said severely enough to offend as the sermon was laced with humor and understanding so the congregation heard the truth and loved him for it. But beneath it lay bitter irony and sarcasm. It was the same irony I heard him use in referring to Aunt Florence's circle in the suburbs, which concentrated on furnishing its houses rather than on making a good home.

People came to my father with their secrets, guilty and otherwise—their troubles with their wives, their troubles with their children, their problems with their businesses. He had gotten to see men close up in a practical way and he did not confuse money or success with brains or virtue.

And yet…and yet he was impressed with money too. Golden took over his father's ice business and turned it into a big coal business which had five hundred employees now. We could detect respect in his voice.

Then there was the fact that the rich men of the congregation kept it going in hard times. Albert Hirsch for instance had built the first edifice on Summer Street and in return it was named after his son Mordecai, hence Congregation Beth Mordecai. I was forty years old before I learned the origin of the Temple name. I had always thought it had been named after Mordecai the hero of the festival of Purim who saved the Jews of Persia from destruction but, no, it had really been named after Hirsch's son—Hirsch who built the Temple on Summer St.

When my father, a bright-eyed aggressive young man fresh from his first congregation in Bridgeport, had come to Perth Amboy, it was 1928. In 1929 came the Crash. In 1930 the temple almost closed its doors and his and the cantor's salaries were cut to the bone. Who had managed to keep the temple open? It was Albert Hirsch who made a massive contribution; Albert had earlier paid off the mortgage on the Summer Street building enabling them to buy the impressive new edifice on Water Street by the bay.

And the organ that resonated through my childhood, the organ that sang "Amen Amen" through every Friday night of my childhood, the organ that gave "There Lives a God" and "Father See thy Supplicant Children" on confirmation days and always punctuated the poetry of the bible. The organ that I hear still behind every idealistic thought, atheist though I imagine myself to be. That organ had been purchased for the temple in 1935 by David Kramer, proprietor of the largest furniture store in town. Without David

Kramer, his furniture, his success, his money, there would be no organ at Temple Beth Mordecai, no "Father See thy Suppliant Children." And Greenfield of the frozen food chain was responsible for the choir loft in which the organ was hidden, giving it a more ethereal quality, since you couldn't see where the enchanted music was coming from.

---

MY FATHER KNEW THAT ALBERT HIRSCH WAS GOOD AT making money and not much else and that his marriage was a shambles and he had a mistress—only the rabbi knew things like that. And he knew David Kramer was a good-enough man with a knack for knowing what furniture would sell next season but who never opened a book and was rather boring to talk to. So he knew what making money did and did not do, but would he still be working if the temple had closed its doors in 1930 without the intervention of Albert Hirsch? And every year the Greenfields made a large contribution, even during the Depression, which kept the temple going. My father's relations with these people was cordial and somewhere deep down, he respected their money.

Of course we had status without money. This is the contradiction of every clergyman's family and when I meet a clergyman's child of any denomination we instantly have an understanding because our childhood shared this singular fact. We did not need to seek status because we already had it and that status did not require money. When I meet a Methodist minister's son we recognize this commonality immediately, it glows across a room. The Methodist minister's son, though he may now be a successful lawyer or writer or engineer, is still wearing a moth-eaten sweater and shoes with holes and socks that do not match because his status does not require money or material things.

My father got along fine with the Greenfields and Kramers and Hirschs. He did not fawn upon them nor did he pay less attention to the less well off majority of the congregation who could not buy organs or pay off mortgages. But he did, I must repeat, get along fine with the Greenfields and Kramers and Hirsches.

And there was Harold Wolf whose father had a gas station, a little gas station which he built into a big oil company. He was impressed. This showed ability and power, to build a gas station into a big oil company which was one of the first to use low sulphur gasoline and which now had a string of gas stations all over the east coast of America. It had refineries near Perth Amboy which refined their own oil and which had its own pipelines carrying in the oil from Texas and had a special relationship with the government of Iran. With this my father was impressed. But he was not impressed that Wolfe spent a lot of time in Vegas and at the dog tracks in Miami. He also could guess at the shenanigans that may have been involved in building the empire, deals cut, throats slashed. He did not discuss these things but we knew he was impressed with Harold Wolf and that at the same time he was not.

Perhaps the gift checks that Harold Wolf sent my father from time to time were put away and invested wisely and became the money my father left us. Harold Wolf was generous with my father. I think, in his mind, my father, the temple and God were closely linked, perhaps even blurred together. This too any Methodist minister's son knows about. Our family received many gifts, we never had money so we could look down our nose at money partly because so much of what we received was IN KIND.

He had, for instance, a courtesy pass to all three movie houses in town—admit One plus Friend. And on Purim great baskets of fruit arrived at our apartment, people liked to send the rabbi fruit on holidays. And we received cream pies from Alice Kweskin, a Sisterhood member who made exquisite pies thick with coconuts, rich with caramel cream. I have never tasted such delicate crusts; these pies arrived on our doorstep on Purim, Hanukkah, and Rosh Hashanah.

And my father never received a parking ticket because the sign in the windshield of our Plymouth, POLICE CHAPLAIN, discouraged any cop from ticketing him for overparking. The windshield in which the POLICE CHAPLAIN sign appeared was the window of a bright blue Plymouth that had appeared with regularity in our back yard every eight years, compliments of the Congregation. Although during the Depression we had a wheezing Whippet that had to be pushed up hills, by the 1940s the bright blue Plymouths had started to appear in our backyard. So we didn't have to buy our own cars. Clothes and furniture were among the items given to the rabbi's family as gifts. It would not be dignified to refuse these gifts. Yet, we still wore hand-me- downs from our cousins, which was why my father could speak with clear-hearted virtue, sarcasm and disapproval of "WE CAN'T GO BACK TO SCHOOL UNTIL WE'VE BEEN TO SAKS FIFTH AVENUE." We were above such things.

This is not to have you think for one minute that my father was a hypocrite, he was not. No, it was not hypocrisy, it was complicated ambivalence.

I think he was privately a socialist of some sort. He didn't talk about it but there was much left over, unspoken but still there from his idealistic youth at the Seminary and before. When he was very old, he was terrified that my mother would be sick and poor when he died and he spent most of his time worrying about his investments in stocks and bonds and poring over the stock market page of the New York Times. He became very knowledgeable about the subject. I think he was a socialist, but at the same time he was watching the stock market carefully and getting a great kick out of it, fascinated by its rises and falls.

Perhaps this was just an old man's fear and insecurity of what would become of his wife when he was gone if he didn't leave her money. But then one wonders for how many years was he afraid? When did the insecurity start? The Stock Market Crash of 1929 came just one year after he arrived in Perth Amboy, the temple lowered his salary and almost had to close its doors and I, their first baby, had just been born. Was my father terrified and insecure ? Did his ambivalence about money start then and there? Money was beneath him, it was materialistic to think about it, but oh dear, what if he didn't have it? What would have happened to him, this promising young rabbi at his first important post ready to prove himself, if the temple had closed its doors that summer of 1931 with a one-year-old baby and an overanxious wife? What would he have done? He had developed no other profession.

The strange thing is that if he was terrified and insecure about money I never knew it. I grew up feeling total security, I did not know his salary had been cut, I never heard any talk of fear or poverty. I remember only the services—the beautiful Friday night services, the stirring sounds of the organ, and all those values that pooh poohed money and looked down upon material things.

While he was reading me poetry and telling me that

books and learning were all that mattered, while he was scoffing at Aunt Florence's crowd for having their homes done by a decorator, was he all this time scared about meeting the next rent? How could this have been kept so hidden from a child? Did my parents discuss it late at night when I was asleep? Was I deaf and blind? How could anti-materialism be conveyed so solidly, so convincingly, if all the while the person speaking was terrified about MONEY? I will never know. I don't think my father really started to feel insecure about the future until my grandfather was mugged. Perhaps that was when the idea of money started to change for him.

My grandfather was a mugging pioneer. He may have been the first person to be mugged in Newark. Two youths mugged him while he was out walking his dog and took his wallet. My grandfather was never the same again and I know it was a sobering and perhaps a life changing experience for my father.

My father had married up both economically and socially. His father was a plumber but he married my mother, whose father was a dental surgeon. My mother's father was a successful dental surgeon and made a great deal of money. My father, at the age of 47, saw that money disappear overnight. My grandfather's hands trembled after the mugging when he handled the dental tools. My helpless grandmother was pressed into service to help him and he soon afterwards had to give it all up and retire. Lo, it turned out that he had saved nothing. All the money he'd earned over the years of dental operations he had spent on expensive suits, dinners out at the Progress Club, vacations, and most important, cards. Worse yet his card game partners, comrades of pleasure as my father put it, seemed to disappear overnight after his trouble, rarely phoning or visiting him. My grandfather hadn't saved a cent and was destitute.

Surely if the temple's nearly closing its doors in his first year in Perth Amboy had not made my father insecure about money, then surely my grandfather's experience did. And this I do remember for by now I was not a small child thrilling to the sonorous tones of the organ. By now I was a college girl and I remember that my father started looking at money in a different way—with fear and insecurity. If Grandpa who earned so much had saved so little, what of other people who had made so much less? He never said this out loud in my hearing but I think perhaps it may have been then that he started squirreling it away.

I do not personally remember my parents denying themselves in those later years. It seems to me they were always eating out at Howard Johnsons and they went on two vacations to Europe. But was he secretly scrimping? Did he deny himself new clothes? Or was he just being a good manager? I still come back to that $200,000. Was it during these years that it accumulated, as my mother fell ill slowly, the Parkinsons falling like a shadow over their lives? My mother first simpering on her tiptoes, then sliding, then falling once in the Howard Johnsons bathroom. Perhaps then the congregation started slipping him envelopes. I know that Harold Wolf, who now sold oil all over the world, sent him a check every year, but I don't know what was in that check. Was it a lot, and did my father save every cent of it? This is important to me. I would like to know because part of that money is now mine.

Was there envy in my father's attitude about money? A young man decides to be a rabbi. He is a smart young man with potential for being a good judge, a fine lawyer, perhaps even a man of affairs and business. But he is studious, he is valedictorian of his high school class, top of his class at NYU, but not admitted to the fraternities because he can't afford to keep up with them. But that's not important to him because young and mustachioed and an ardent idealistic follower of Woodrow Wilson he knows those things are not important. It is the life of the mind that is important. He becomes interested in history, literature, and philosophy. He had earlier thought of becoming a rabbi because he was studious and was raised in a religious family. Now he thinks of it again because he is inspired by some of the modern contemporary movements in Judaism. He decides to enroll in the Seminary, not the Orthodox one of his parents, but the Conservative one of contemporary thinking modern folks. And he shines at the Seminary and he becomes president of his class and he graduates at the top of his class. He has found soulmates and intellectual equals, he has found a life of the intellect in which he can feel at home—a life of idealism. Here money plays no part.

But when he goes out in the world he slowly discovers that there are small congregations and larger congregations and largest congregations. The most brilliant rabbis—or not necessarily the most brilliant but the most able in some way—will climb to the biggest congregations, the richest congregations in Long Island. There is after all even in the realm of pure thought a pecking order among rabbis too.

When he arrives at his second congregation, though he is loved there, it is not the largest but it is large enough, and it is large enough to make one's name and reputation in. He decides not to strive to go beyond it, but rather to make his home right here.

His prestige comes slowly but it comes not only in his growing popularity and respect in the congregation and community but beyond it as well—first president of the state synagogue council, then chairman of committees on the national level. He becomes active in national rabbinical work. During the war he heads a committee that ministers to chaplains of the armed services and in the course of this stimulating work he travels to many air bases and meets colonels and generals of different faiths He wins the respect of his rabbinical colleagues because of his diplomatic skills and his ability to chair a meeting fairly, and he finds himself elected to the presidency of the national rabbis organization. His picture is taken with President Truman, another with President Eisenhower. His congregation back home sees his picture with Truman with Eisenhower and they are proud their rabbi, their dear rabbi, is nationally important too.

So who needs money? One is paid off in prestige and status which all people need and which money is usually just a standing for. In his city he is loved, and in his congregation loved, and in his family loved. He conducts our family Seders with beauty, his personality is charismatic, he is the leader of the family.

Just as my grandfather was a pioneer in the field of mugging, so my two aunts were pioneers in suburbia. While we lived in dirty industrial Perth Amboy, the sky always black with smoke from oil refineries and National Lead, they lived in a grassland suburb with cute white shuttered one-family houses and lawns. Aunt Florence had a hammock in her backyard, they had gleaming modern kitchens where my Uncle Ben made fudge on Sundays. My father loved my mother' s sisters and their husbands and they revered him, yet rarely would a visit to the suburbs pass but that he would make some sarcastic remark on the country club crowd, the home furnishing preoccupation, the importance attached to clothes. Was it envy? Was it macho? Or was it genuine disapproval of suburban materialism?

Did it sometimes seem to him that he must prove himself as a man by providing his wife with the material things her sisters had? Surely my mother herself never made the comparison, but he was a short man of five foot three. You never noticed it because he was so charismatic. My mother thought of him as ten feet high, as most people did. But maybe, on those days when he felt five foot three, despite all his contempt for materialism, perhaps he felt my mother felt he should be able to give her a house with a cathedral ceiling.

One thing is certain he did not want us children to want what our cousins had, and we didn't want it. Ever. Not even when we grew up and had families of our own. When my father's will was read and his safe deposit box was opened, disclosing all those stocks and bonds, our first impulse was Aunt Florence mustn't know. The Anecksteins mustn't know. The congregation mustn't know. It would tarnish our family image. It would degrade us, reduce us, diminish us all if it became known that we had money.

# 10

# Wives and Daughters

When my father was seventy-eight years old, bowed by arthritis and heart disease but still a member of the board of directors of Perth Amboy General Hospital, he remarked: "You know, two of the leading women of the ladies' auxiliary are asking for places on the hospital's board of directors, and the men won't let them in. These two women are brighter, more capable than most of the men on the board, but the men just won't admit them. Amazing conservatism!"

The remark, made in 1976, reflected a lifelong recognition of the potential competencies of women. I was raised in the light of this insight: when I was twelve and had won the Passaic Junior Girls' Tennis Tournament by defeating Louise, Margie, Barbara and Anne, all hopelessly unathletic, he had written me from a trip: "Try to play tennis, from now on, with the boys or the older girls so that way you'll improve." He didn't want me to lie back and rest on my laurels. I must improve my game by pitting myself against the boys, must not take Louise for my standard.

I was raised to be smart and capable and strong, as one would raise a boy. And yet... he never applied these standards to my mother. He had one set of expectations for his daughter, another for his wife. The potentialities of women were for other women, not for Lillian, his lovable, adorable, beautiful wife. She was not expected, or encouraged, to develop herself.

And after my mother had been so reduced, when I was a teenager he turned to me for conversation and stimulation; and my mother sat silently at the kitchen table and listened to our talk. What was she thinking? She never seemed jealous. She always seemed to be wondering whether the pot roast was done, as we debated Descartes. Did she resent us? I don't think so. They had a passionate marriage; their early love letters (which we found later) show it, and the little notes she tucked into his pajamas whenever he went away on trips. (A five-day trip to an army base, where my father, a clergyman, visited servicemen during World War II, was treated as a family tragedy; she was so lonely and helpless and unprotected alone, constantly congratulated by letter for doing so well all by herself, with the children. And his longing notes of missing her: "Tonight, I will pretend that my pillow is Lillian… Only three days now until I return…")

When my mother was young she was musical. She played the piano unusually well, and her teacher felt she might become a concert pianist. My father, on the other hand, was completely unmusical, he had a tin ear, and after they were married there was rarely music in the house. For a while we had a piano, and she played the wedding march at occasional weddings in our home. But she rarely played; and finally the piano was sold. They never went to concerts. She lost her ability to play. Her one great childhood interest had been discouraged, doused.

My mother was shy and retiring and the idea of being

a "rabbi's wife," a leader in temple functions, had terrified her from the beginning, and had caused her only hesitation in deciding to marry him. He didn't mind; in fact, he preferred her being in the background, an unobtrusive voice in the temple choir (not Dorothy Marshall's thrilling, conspicuous soprano at the front of the choir loft). And he liked her sitting in the back of the Women's Guild meeting when he gave his book reviews, silently cheering him on, not the pushy president or the capable treasurer or the busy organizer of the church bazaar. Organizations were not her thing? That was just fine with him.

Housework was considered too much for my mother; we had a series of Polish maids (all named Anna), who vacuumed and hung the clothes out on the line. My father seemed to consider housework a herculean effort for my mother and helped her as much as he could. It was he who, once a week, gathered up all the sheets and shirts and pillowcases into a pile in the middle of the kitchen floor (this was considered too heavy for my mother), tied them up in a sheet, carried the bundle down the stairs, and drove it to the laundry. He had to drive, for my mother never learned to drive and he didn't encourage her to learn. Whenever she went anywhere he drove her there, waited for her, picked her up and drove her home. He grew stronger. She grew weaker, less capable. Meanwhile he was raising his daughter to push her limits.

From the day I was born my father considered me something special, remarkable. I was hung over and doted upon and expected to succeed. He yearned for my achievements. I was a remarkable and incredible human being. Was I? Or was I merely an invention of my father, an extension of his intense will?

Eagerly he wrote down my first words. "Judy's first two hundred words" are listed proudly in my Baby Book. Clearly a remarkable person.

When I was three he read me poetry at bedtime: tragic, beautiful, haunting poetry, "Annabelle Lee," "The Bells," "Little Boy Blue." Naturally I began to like poetry and soon began to write some. He thought my poems remarkable. Were they?

He brought home books, when I was four, and encouraged me to read them. He took me to the library. As I grew bigger, I started to run and play with the boys, climb fences, play softball. I sped down the hills on my sled, learned to ride a bike. In this my father encouraged me; he smiled upon all signs of verve and energy and resourcefulness. Let me run!

My mother worried about all this; shouldn't I be playing with dolls as she had at my age? It became known that, at my age, she had had a headless doll, which she'd loved all the more because of its deformity. Why wasn't I playing with dolls? But his was the stronger spirit, the clearer vision… and so, my mother gave up and just made sure I had taken my vitamins (as Carlton Fredericks, the radio nutritionist, had advised), and was bundled up warm, and she let me run and climb. With some misgivings. My father had no misgivings. He had one image for his daughter, another for his wife.

While my mother was in the hospital giving birth to my sister, when I was in kindergarten, he took me to the barber shop with him and got us both haircuts. My hair was cut short. When I put my blue wool cap over it, I looked like a little boy. We visited my mother in the hospital. She had just given birth and was worn out and nervous. She took one look at me and burst into tears. "Oh Max: How could you?"

I have a picture of me, in a row of other kindergarten children. I do stand out with my blue wool cap over my ears, crouched as if ready to run. I look tough — like a street kid.

I sat in my room and wrote stories. My father raved about them. How good: How precocious: Were they? He showed them proudly to his friends.

As I started high school, the scribbling turned naturally toward journalism. My father no doubt feared that I, entering puberty, might lose my ambition and sense of direction, might opt for mere girlhood. Casually one evening, when I was a freshman in high school, starting to eye the handsome football players, he remarked: "Have you thought of trying out for the school paper?"

"What would I do, Dad?" (Still thinking of Harrison, the quarterback.)

"Why not go down to the guidance office and find out what became of last year's graduates? It might make for an interesting story..."

It was the only push he ever gave me on journalism, but was enough to spark a meteoric high school journalism career. I did go to the guidance office (ogling Harrison in the hall). There had been a study of what last year's graduates were doing now. I did write a story about it and earned recognition as an enterprising freshman journalist. From there, it was all uphill: interviewing visiting band leaders, writing a monthly column, finally becoming editor of the high school paper. My father was so proud. He'd always known I would go far.

I turned sixteen. I started to question everything: life, religion, politics. He always urged me to look things up, find the answers, reach my own conclusions. He encouraged my seeking; he wanted an inquiring mind he could bounce his thoughts off of.

I grilled him on our religion. Was there a God? HOW did we know? Why were religions necessary? Why were the first-born Egyptian children killed in the Bible story; weren't they innocents? Why did we need all this mumbo-jumbo anyway?

He encouraged my rebellion, enjoyed it. He wanted me to use my brain: to be a bold, independent, questioning kind of person. We had long debates, discussions, and arguments at the kitchen table.

My mother was not included in these discussions. He never discussed ideas with her; he assumed she wouldn't be interested. He talked to me, was interested in what I had to say. Pygmalion and Galatea.

Did she feel left out, excluded? Freud would say yes but I say no. I don't think she minded when we debated Descartes and nobody asked her opinion. She was used to not being asked. She was just as happy to be out of it. As long as I ate her spinach. As long as Dad cut down on the potatoes... he was putting on weight, and it worried her. So, while we debated life and literature and religion, she worried about the starches and sugars we were getting, and she planned to buy a new dress for Passover, one Max would admire her in.

Everything was all right between them. When they looked at each other, no child could have missed it.

If she was sick, he took care of her tenderly. If he had some skirmish, some insult at temple, she was balm to his wounds: just by her certainty, her unshakable, uncritical certainty that he was totally right, that he was six feet tall. (Actually he was five foot three, but not to her.)

She was raised to be a child-woman, a child-wife, just as her mother had been. My mother's mother, our "Mama", was married to a dentist and was expected to carry no responsibility. She was loving and light-headed; she often went shopping at Woolworth's and got so absorbed in her shopping that she wasn't home in time to make supper. All forgave her. She was so loving, so sweet, so pretty: her thick, lustrous grey hair, I can see it now, I used to brush it out at night whenever she came to our house for an overnight visit. Her husband, too, had babied her, loved her tenderly, did everything to smooth away the cares, to relieve her of responsibility and care. She too had her Annas to clean the house and hang out the clothes, but in Newark they were Marys or Marias instead of Annas, girls who would grow up knowing responsibility. If Mama had had a drunken husband to cope with, she might have grown up. But she had a loving dentist who smoothed everything over, who took the family out to the Progress Club for pancakes if supper wasn't ready. And she looked up at Pa, her husband, for his many successes: member of the Newark Board of Education, head of the free dental clinic of Newark. In this family, the women compiled scrapbooks about their husbands' accomplishments and pored over them, and she showed hers proudly to the children: Pa is a leader in the community: See, Pa is so sought after as an after-dinner speaker: She was beautiful, loving, and scatter-brained; she raised her two daughters, Lillian and Rose, with the help of many Marys and Marias.

Only one thing about my grandmother, though. She couldn't take loud noises. They made her nervous. When she visited us overnight, she couldn't sleep because she always complained that Mrs. Fisher, in the apartment above, was moving furniture around all night long. It was true that there were occasional faint noises from the Fishers' radio. But to Nana they were deafening. She was delicate, high-strung; noises gave her a headache. Then, I would have to brush her lustrous, beautiful grey hair to drive the headache away.

But most of the time Mama was happy and light-hearted. "I have just had a kaffee klatch, all by myself," wrote Mama to her daughter Lillian, using the German phrases that peppered their conversation. "Do you ever do that, Lillian?" She was always worrying that her Lillian was working too hard.

This was the Lillian that my father married, and this was the wife he wanted; and after he married her he discouraged any attempt on her part to grow up, to expand or develop or become stronger. But it was in love and tenderness that he did this.

Still, my father had another image of womanhood: his own mother. Tough Bessie Davidson. Pushy, a leader among women. An organizer. Single-handedly started a Home for the Aged when she discovered there was none in Trenton. Later, single- handedly ran a rooming house on the Jersey shore, a busy rooming house of summer guests spilling over the porches. Her plumber husband leaned on her. A strong, resourceful, pushy woman. My father carried this mother in his head. But he'd married my mother—sheltered, loving, beautiful Lillian—to be protected and taken care of. And take care of her, tenderly, he did, to his dying day.

There was something—something I did not know of—something from long, long ago that held them together. Something deeper than Descartes, stronger than sex. It had to do, I think, with their earliest days together in his first congregation, in New Brunswick, before he came to Perth Amboy. He'd been a fresh, brash, ambitious young rabbi, fresh out of seminary, not knowing how to handle a congregation. I never did know what happened there, why he left; it happened before I was born. But something during that period had cemented them forever. It was, I think, that he was under fire, unsure of himself, attacked, criticized, and she'd stood by him with utter, unswerving, uncritical, unquestioning devotion and faith.

He was six feet tall—then and forever. That is how she saw him. She was already starting to compile her scrapbook on him, and his achievements, just as her mother had of Pa.

Meanwhile our kitchen conversations had turned me into a complete rebel, and when it was time for me to go to college, and I was admitted to the University of Chicago, which would have taken me far away and out of his control, my father got worried. He convinced himself that, if I went to the University of Chicago, I would come back a Communist. He wanted to have a little more oversight than that.

So—with all my vaunted independence of mind and thought and action, I was persuaded (the price was lower, it was a good school, I had a scholarship) to attend a college twelve miles from home.

Inspired by my father, I did brilliantly at college. At high school my marks had been ordinary: my claim to fame had been my writings. But at college, by intensive effort and strenuous overachievement, I studied hard and got the highest marks in the school. I shone scholastically. I made Phi Beta Kappa. But I did not become a Communist, and I did not break away.

How proud he was of my success, my achievement: How proud of the Phi Beta Kappa key: How proud of his brilliant daughter: She would go far.

Three years later, I married an engineer. My father, I know, was pleased that I had married a good provider.

After my marriage, my father never once asked me what I was reading, or what I was writing, or what ambitions I had for my life.

I was now a wife, not a daughter.

# 11

# I Am Waiting for Three Men

When I was young, men came flocking to my door. Now I'm 38 and they don't.

Today I'm sitting in my house all day waiting for three men to come and visit me. And I fear that not one of them will come.

My husband knows nothing of this. He thinks I'm at the Graduate School of Continuing Education studying the population explosion in Tanzania. But actually, I'm home, waiting all day.

Waiting for three men to come.

The first man is the Rug Installer.

Last month a rug was installed in my living room. But the men didn't put a runner on the stairs as they were supposed to do with the leftover material.

The men left abruptly last month saying: "Well we installed your rug. We didn't put the runner on the stairs, but we'll be back tomorrow to do it."

"Why didn't you put a runner on the stairs?" I asked politely. Actually I didn't even care about the runner. I've always found runners rather affected. But it was in the agreement, and my husband loves runners.

"The tacks are the wrong color," they said mysteriously.

"But we'll be back the first thing in the morning."

They never came back. I waited for them faithfully for nine days, missing classes on the shortage of water in Manchuria and the quality of the environment in Burma. But they never came back. Finally I called Boris, the man at the carpet store who sold me the rug. "May I speak to Boris ?" I asked.

Boris insists that we call him Boris. I'm not sure if it's his first name or his last name. Actually I feel it's a little presumptuous of us to call him Boris when we hardly know him. But Boris insisted on it when we bought the carpet. He said it would make our relationship more lasting and personal.

"Boris," I said. "This is Judy Chasek in Stamford."

"I hope you're happy with your new red wool rug," said Boris.

"It's blue polyester, Boris." I said.

"Oh yes," said Boris vaguely.

"It's just lovely, Boris." I said. "Only, I'm still waiting for the men to come back to install the runner on the stairs. You know, with the leftover material, like you promised?"

"Oh yes," said Boris vaguely.

"The men said they'd come back the next day but they didn't and..."

"What were their names?" asked Boris.

"Whose?"

"The men."

"Gosh, I don't know, Boris. I thought you'd...."

"What did they look like? Think: What did they look like?

"Can you remember what they looked like?"

"I don't know. Pretty ordinary, I'd say. Twenty-five years old, no, maybe 30. They smoked a lot. The shorter one had a skin condition."

It developed that Boris had no contact whatsoever with the installers. They operated out of an entirely different office in Glassboro, New Jersey, and Boris had never laid eyes on any of them. He didn't know their names. He didn't know their phone number. Their two organizations were not in touch.

"Boris, could you please find them?" I said.

"I'll call you back," said Boris.

He never called back. I stayed home five days, waiting for his call, but he never called back. The following week, however, I received a pleasant post card from a man named Charles in Glassboro, New Jersey, who said he hoped his installation of my carpet was satisfactory and he could be reached in Glassboro, New Jersey at 441-0022, area code 609.

I called the number. Charles was very polite. Although he had a slight case of amnesia (couldn't recall installing any carpet, could not recall any runner, could not recall sending any post card), he said he would be happy to get it all straightened out with the carpet store and would phone me right back.

Seven days later Boris called.

"I hear you're giving the carpet installers a hard time," he said.

"A hard time?"

"They say you're raising a big rumpus insisting that the stairs be covered wall to wall. Didn't I tell you I can't do this Mrs. Chasek. There's not enough leftover material to cover your stairs wall to wall."

"But I don't *want* them covered wall to wall: I just want a runner down the middle..."

"The men said you insisted on wall to wall and that's why they left without doing the stairs."

"But I didn't. That's not why they left. It was something about the color of the tacks. Actually I don't even *want* a runner…"

"Well, you gotta have one," said Boris severely. " It's in the agreement, I'll call you back."

"Boris, could you give me some idea when you might call…?"

It was too late. I heard a click.

Five days later, Charles called.

"We'll be there Thursday," said Charles.

"Charles," I cried, "do you mean this coming Thursday?" It was too late. The phone clicked.

So Charles is one of the men I'm waiting for today. Another is the Salvation Army man.

When the men installed my new rug they took off the old rug. They rolled it up and placed it outside my front door. I was planning to put an ad in the Used Rug Column of the newspaper only I changed my mind when I heard one rug installer say to another….

"God this is a crummy looking rug."

I didn't think it was such a crummy looking rug. I was rather attached to it. To be frank, in certain ways I liked it better than my new rug. But since the installing men looked down on it like that I felt embarrassed putting it in the Used Rug Column. I had visions of dozens upon dozens of perfect strangers trooping past my door every night murmuring, "God what a crummy looking rug!" It reminded me of a recurrent dream I'd had as a child. So, instead, I decided with a magnanimous flourish, to give the rug away to the Salvation Army.

I called the Salvation Army and was thrilled when the man said Yes, they certainly could use a large beige rug and they would be by for it on their truck call in my neighborhood tomorrow.

I felt wonderful: efficient and virtuous at the same time. I would get a heavy rug carted off my front lawn. And someone would get a nice rug, free.

The next day came and went. I stayed home from Graduate School which is why I now know absolutely nothing about the educational system in Tunisia. But the Salvation Army man never came.

Nor the next day. Nor the next. I phoned. Oh yes they were going to pick it up tomorrow, they said.

Weeks passed. The rolled-up rug outside my front door was rained on. It was snowed on. Mildew formed. "Why is this rotten old rug still curled up outside the door?" my husband snarled some time during the third week. "This certainly is a poorly run household: If someone at the plant functioned like this we'd fire him!"

I tried to hold onto my temper, "It's the business," I told myself. "Sales are down. He's depressed. Don't take it personally." I'm taking a psychology course Monday nights at the community college which is helping me cope with situations like this in a mature understanding way.

But day after day as I kept calling the Salvation Army, and they kept saying they'd come and they didn't come, I became more and more depressed. I felt more and more rejected.

"I'm giving away a rug and no one will take it," I thought. "I'm giving it away and no one will take it."

About the fourth week a terrible suspicion began to dawn on me.

Perhaps the Salvation Army man had come by in his truck when I wasn't looking and had looked at the rug and thought it wasn't worth carting away.

And they kept pretending they had not come yet because they didn't want to hurt my feelings.

The more I thought about it, the more likely it seemed. I recalled the Salvation Army men's faces shaking tambourines in front of Gimbels at Christmas. Their kind, merciful expressions. Yes, it was just the sort of thing they might do. They were too kind to tell me how they felt about my rug so they were stringing me along.

Just yesterday, I called the Salvation Army again. Again they said oh, yes, the man would be in my neighborhood tomorrow, he'd probably pick it up then, thank you very much. And although it's been so long, I can't help thinking maybe he really will come today.

So the Salvation Army man is the second man I'm waiting for today.

The third is the gas station man who has my car.

This morning while I was washing the breakfast dishes, my twelve year old daughter Allison returned home from the school bus stop. She'd fallen while walking to the bus stop and bruised her knee. I had to doctor her knee, and by the time I was done she had missed the school bus. I would have to drive her to school.

We got in the car. The car wouldn't start.

"If I'm going to be late, I won't go," said Allison. "It's embarrassing to be late to school."

"You'll go," I said firmly, "I just have to call Jim Barrett. He'll get the car started."

I called Jim Barrett, our neighborhood service station operator. Jim used to just work at the gas station and was always considered a hale, good-natured fellow with a warm smile as well as an expert mechanic. There is one woman in our neighborhood, in fact, who did her psychology master's thesis on Jim to determine how a person could grow up in Our Society and still be SO Pleasant and Happy and Well Adjusted.

Only, Jim started to change shortly after the thesis was written. When the old gas station owner retired he sold the gas station to Jim, and then Jim had to start worrying about paying the light and gas and sending out bills and making people pay bills and things like that. Now, Jim wasn't so pleasant anymore. There was a worry line on his brow. He didn't crack jokes. He was developing a slight nervous twitch. The strangest part of all, he didn't fix cars as well anymore. When you get your car fixed, the following week the same thing is usually not working again.

Well, anyway, I called Jim and he rushed over in his red tow truck and looked under the hood of my car.

"Jim," I said, "Allison's late to school and I have to drive her. Do you think you might be able to fix it quickly so I can get her to school?"

"Oh sure, no problem!" said Jim in his old jovial way, peering out from under the hood. "It doesn't look serious at all, Alison will be in school in no time! We wouldn't want Allison to miss any school." He chucked Allison under the chin and drove off in his red truck towing my car behind him.

"That's funny," I remarked to Allison. "Funny he couldn't fix it here if it's not serious. Towing costs a lot."

"That's all right," said Allison, who had curled up on the sofa with her latest library book. *The Girl who Had No Boy Friends*. "He can take as long as he likes as far as I'm concerned."

"While we're waiting for Jim to bring the car back you should be studying your biology young lady," I said. "Don't you have a biology test today?"

"I'm not going to school," said Allison. "It's already 9: 30 and I've already missed one subject. It's ridiculous to go to school when one subject is already over." "You're going," I said. "I'm not," she said.

An hour ticked by. Two hours. Three. It was 12:30. Nobody had come. Not the rug installer. Not the Salvation Army man. Not Jim Barrett.

I phoned the rug installer in Glassboro, New Jersey, but there was no answer. I phoned the Salvation Army and they said the truck was on the road. I phoned the gas station, but Jim couldn't come to the phone. They said he was in conference.

"Are you waiting for somebody mom?" asked Allison, turning a page in *The Girl who Had No Boy Friends.*

"NO."

"Why are you pacing up and down?"

"Who's pacing?"

I felt exasperation rising in me. I didn't want Allison home today. I didn't want Allison here while I waited all day long for three men to come to my house—three men who would probably never come. It seemed like such a forlorn, pathetic, mortifying way for a person to spend a day. I didn't want Allison to witness it with her sharp knowing eyes.

At one o'clock I said, "I'm sure Jim will be along any minute with the car. Start getting ready for school,"

"You must be crazy," said Allison. "I've already missed Spanish, Mathematics and Science. There is no point going to school when you've already missed three classes. Nobody does it. I'd be so embarrassed. Nobody does it. "

"What do you mean nobody?" I said. "I, myself, was always late to school as a child."

It was true. I had never told anyone before. I suddenly remembered myself a small lone figure hurrying down Paterson St. toward PS 7 while, in the distance, I could hear the ominous tolling of the Third Bell.

"Judy was late to school because she dawdled." I remembered my mother's pencilled notes.

Dawdled. The word came echoing back over the years with a sickening ring.

Perhaps, then, I have always been incompetent, ineffectual, wasteful, I thought with sinking heart. If I weren't, why would I be sitting around a house all day waiting for three men who refuse to come?

I phoned the gas station again. This time I got Jim. He sounded vaguely irritated to hear from me. He had not sounded that way in the old days before he bought the gas station, in the old days when they were writing that thesis about him.

"Jim, this is Judy Chasek," I said.

"Oh," said Jim.

"Allison's missed several of her classes," I said, "and I was just wondering when my car might be ready."

"Who missed her classes?" asked Jim. I could hear a lot of banging in the background.

"Allison," I said.

"Oh," said Jim. I could tell he didn't recall who Allison was.

"Have you found out what's wrong with the car?" I asked.

"Haven't gotten to it yet," he said brusquely.

"Do you have any idea when you might?"

"Oh, some time today. Maybe tomorrow. Saturday at the latest."

He hung up.

I sat down by the phone. That is where I'm sitting now, thinking.

101

Will Jim Barrett come today?
Will the Rug installer come today?
Will the Salvation Army man come today?
I hope so. I truly hope so. When I was young, men came flocking to my door.

# 12

# The Visit

When we were kids my father would read us the *Little Boy Blue* poem, little suspecting how prescient it would be for his latter years. My father was short with large blue eyes. The children's poem, written by Eugene Field, read:

> *...Time was when the little toy dog was new,*
> *And the soldier was passing fair;*
> *And that was the time when our Little Boy Blue*
> *Kissed them and put them there.*

> *"Now, don't you go till I come," he said,*
> *"And don't you make any noise!"*
> *So, toddling off to his trundle-bed,*
> *He dreamt of the pretty toys;*
> *And, as he was dreaming, an angel song*
> *Awakened our Little Boy Blue—*
> *Oh! the years are many, the years are long,*
> *But the little toy friends are true!*

> *Still, faithful to Little Boy Blue they stand,*
> *Each in the same old place—*

*Awaiting the touch of a little hand,*
*The smile of a little face...*

My mother in her early 70s gradually fell ill to non-specific maladies and my father, unable to tend to her, was forced to place her in an intensive care nursing home. She was completely bedridden. There was no prognosis. My father visited her daily. He brought chocolate ice cream and spoon fed it to her. He knew she loved chocolate ice cream. It's her only pleasure now. He seemed to keep her alive by the sheer force of his presence, his will, his love, and the ice cream.

But as the years passed he grew less strong. His heart and legs became weak. His diabetes resulted in gangrene beginning to nibble at his big toe. It became a herculean expenditure of sheer will to keep coming.

One day he stopped coming. He has been rushed to the hospital with heart failure. Mother cannot articulate the missed visits rationally. Time is a vague thing to her. Days fade into weeks. She does not consciously think, where is Max? She doesn't know how long it's been since his last visit. No one tells her that Max is also bedridden, but her body knows that he is gone.

She begins to refuse food. A tube is inserted into her nose, through which nourishment is fed directly to her stomach. She has lost the will to live. The tube keeps her alive, but the tube doesn't spoon feed her chocolate ice cream and hold her hand. We visit her weekly but are helpless.

Meanwhile my father is brought home and we engage a full-time nurse's aide to care for him. His mind has begun to fade. He knows only one thing, he must make financial arrangements. He sits in his bed going distractedly through his checkbooks and other personal papers. He knows that he must do something for someone, but what and for whom? He worries about who will take care of mother after he dies.

Meanwhile a miracle happens. Mother begins to eat again. She begins to sit up and is daily brought to the sun room in a wheelchair. She sits there day after day, week after week, awaiting visitors, but whom she is not clear.

What has become of her little boy blue?

Meanwhile my father in a moment of restored vigor announces that he must see mother again. We are not sure what to do but he convinces us he can manage a visit. We rent a wheelchair, bring him to the car, and whisk him off to the nursing home.

At the nursing home mother is sitting in her wheelchair in the sun room. We wheel father in. They sit for a while each in their own wheelchair, side by side, saying nothing. Then he reaches out for her hand and holds it for a few moments. Mother smiles. That is the last time they will ever see each other again. My father died not long after.

*Still faithful to the little boy blue*
*they stand each in the same old place*
*Awaiting the touch of the little hand*
*the smile of the little face.*

# 13

# The Ride

The heavy burden of my mother. Visiting her every weekend, at her home. Sometimes, when I come, she is sitting up in her hospital-type bed beneath the large, posed, "official" picture of my father. My father in his prime, arms folded, the photographer has placed the light in such a way that he looks like an important, distinguished figure. Not the father we all knew and loved, gathering up the dirty laundry in a pile to help my mother. No, a sanitized, official, distinguished, meeting-with-President-Eisenhower father. The picture hangs over her bed, above her head, behind her. But she doesn't see it, because she cannot turn her head. She is 81, and an invalid.

Visiting her; trying to carry on a conversation if she is awake, as she lies in her hospital bed with the radio beside her playing the soft, comfortable, popular songs of her generation. Or, watching Mrs. Appersley spoon delicious chicken and peas into her mouth, followed by an appetizing brownie. Or, on days when she's reasonably awake and alert, coaxing her into singing with me all the old familiar songs she still likes to sing: "Nearer my God," "Amazing Grace."

The burden of driving two hours there and two hours back to visit her every weekend and usually she is asleep anyway. The burden of keeping Mrs. Appersley, the nurse, happy and content and entertained so that she won't run back to South Carolina. The burden of assuring my sister Lois that of course we don't mind that they can't visit as often. My sister's husband Ted cherishes his weekends off from teaching school to build the addition to his house. He is building a glass addition, very contemporary, which is flooded with light and will be the studio he dreams of painting in.

—————————

ON THE DAY OF OUR MOTHER'S FUNERAL I AM A LITTLE concerned about my sister. She hadn't been with Mother much at the end. I don't want my sister to feel guilty; there's nothing to be gained from it. As we get into the hearse, after the funeral service, for the long ride to the cemetery, I try to detect any sign of guilt or self-flagellation in my sister. I cannot. By the end of the ride, it is I who am filled with guilt.

It all started as we reminisced about our childhood, about our mother and father, as we sit in the back seat of the hearse on the way to the cemetery:

"At least they'll be lying side by side for eternity, just as they would have wanted," I remark. "I'm so glad, aren't you, that when Dad died we left half of the tombstone blank for Mother's inscription? They'll be on one tombstone: They're together again."

Together again. I think, for the hundredth time, of their perfect marriage… of her devotion to him, her idolization of him, of his intellect, his achievements, his character… and of his devotion to her, the passionate letters of their early courtship; of his years of doing for her, picking her up everywhere because she never learned to drive, their little love notes tucked in suitcases when he went on a rare professional trip, her scrapbooks full of clippings of his triumphs. I think of his admiration of her great beauty, and as it faded, the good trips they had together to Europe and Mexico, their happy letters home, then the sadder hints starting, Mother feeling a little tired during a trip to Paris, a visit to the doctor, "Just having trouble getting over the flu," its persistence, her first suggestion of Parkinson's Disease, her step beginning to falter, the rigid gait, the cogwheeling of the hands, her first terrified realization that she was walking the way Ruth Kimball used to walk, the first signs of mental deterioration, her inability to get up in the morning, to choose which dress she wished to wear, deliberating for hours between the green and the blue, Dad's patience, his devotion, his depression… his lovely wife turning into a sickly, muddle-headed, confused invalid; his never-altering love and dedication, their drives to Florida, the time their parked car started to roll at a gas station with her inside it, how he'd run and stopped the car with the force of his body and then driven all the way to Florida without admitting his leg was broken…

Then, the final agonized necessity of the nursing home, how he bribed the nurses shamelessly with chocolates to take special care of his darling wife, his daily visits to the nursing home, brushing her still lustrous gray hair as he pushed her down the halls in her wheelchair; his final illness, his insistence on visiting the nursing home every day even after he could barely walk because of the diabetes and the gangrene which had settled in one foot; trudging up the front stairs of the nursing home, with her favorite, chocolate ice cream. I think about the time she stopped eating and he was afraid she might die and he coaxed the chocolate ice cream into her mouth every day, a little at a time, telling her a story as he fed it, to distract her, and she pulled out of it and soon they were able to take the tube out of her nose and he was oh, so ecstatically happy; and he kept coming though it was freezing cold, now, and the gangrene was turning a different color, only he concealed it from his doctor because he was afraid the doctor would order him not to visit the nursing home, since now it was February and cold with slippery snow. How he came every day and pushed her down the hall in her wheelchair and she was still his beloved, dearest, and he pushed her to the room where some of the livelier patients were gazing at color TV, and they watched it together, in companionable silence, though she couldn't really follow it; and then one day he couldn't make it up the front stairs anymore, he had heart failure, and even though his mind was starting to get confused, he knew one thing: he must get everything ready so that his beloved wife would be protected after his death with a marital trust which would care of her, always.

And how his plan had worked, had worked so well that after his death the trust was enough to care for her comfortably, so well in fact that she was able to leave the nursing home and return to her own home with a round-the-clock nurse...all these things pass through my mind as we ride to the cemetery in the hearse while my Aunt Florence, in the front seat, chats about how she isn't sure whether she wants to be buried next to her first or second husband, and my Aunt Betsy gingerly lets it be known that she would like to have the green, crystal vase.

"At least they'll be side by side, forever, now" I say to my sister, "as they'd want to be. It's a comfort to know that, even though the last few years have been so hard for her, she had what few women have, a perfect marriage to someone who loved her heart and soul."

"You think of them as having a happy marriage?" my sister says.

"Of course. Don't you?"

"My memories of childhood are full of fighting and screaming. And of his ignoring her to talk to you."

"Full of fights and screaming? Well, she was high-strung and emotional…and there was that thyroid condition she had when I was small…were you born, then, yet? I guess the house was noisy, when we were kids. I do remember lots of shouting. But the whole apartment was noisy, Lois. Don't you remember, the Fishers always shouting, you could hear things so well through the thin walls, and Mrs. Bellamy upstairs always moving furniture around so loudly in the middle of the night, and oh yes, Mrs. Chadash and Mrs. Weiss always yelling to each other across the alley, in Hungarian. 'CHADASH NENNY! "

The hearse lurches around a corner. I smile to myself, remembering. The memory was a fond one, a happy one.

"No, I mean fighting and screaming. At each other. I remember a lot of that, from as far back as I can remember. I remember Mommy crying a lot. I always felt sorry for her. She was always crying a lot."

"Crying? I don't remember her crying, at all." I rack my brain for such recollection, cannot locate it at all. "Are you sure? Crying a lot? Why? Of course, you were six years younger than I…"

"I'm not sure why. But I remember she cried a lot and I was sorry for her…"

"They quarreled sometimes about us, I guess. Yes, I remember some of that. But mainly I remember Mommy giggling. Do you remember, at weddings? And at temple, sometimes, during the solemn parts? I remember the two of them laughing a lot together..." In fact, just before he had to put her in the nursing home, I suddenly remember my father saying wistfully: "You know, yesterday Mom giggled and it almost sounded the way she used to giggle... It sounded like her old laugh. It..." His face was alight, remembering the sound.

"But they never talked about anything together," my sister says. "You were his intellectual companion, not Mother. I remember all those times sitting around the supper table, Mommy not saying a word while you and Dad talked about philosophy or politics..."

"It's true they didn't share intellectual interests. But I don't think it mattered. If he had wanted an intellectual woman, he would have married one."

"But how do you think she felt when she was left out of all those conversations you two had about books? They were usually books she hadn't read! You two would talk for hours. It was always you he was talking to, not her. she must have felt terrible. I remember I felt so sorry for her."

I search my memory. Yes, I remember those talks, when I was a teenager, and even in later life. We had shared interests that he and Mom hadn't had. I had never thought she minded. She hadn't seemed to... Hadn't she always encouraged our talks, beamed upon them? I remember vaguely, uneasily, a long conversation my father and I once had about the Marshall Plan while my mother was clearing the table....had she felt left out?

"You stole Dad from Mother," my sister says. "I always felt so sorry for her. I remember her as being so sad."

"Sad? But he always treated her like a queen! He adored her! She knew it."

"Maybe she didn't know it."

"Of course she did."

Snapshots of my mother, at various ages, pass in succession through my mind. Pictures I'd seen in family albums; of a child, a young woman, a bride. In all these photographs she wore a passive, pensive, yes a somewhat sad expression. Worried, I had thought. Even as a young girl, the photographs suggested, before she was married, before she'd met my father, my mother had been basically worried.

"I know she was worrisome," I say slowly, "and when she lost her first baby — it was born so healthy and then somehow sickened and died -— I know this was a great blow to her and it was a long time before they had another.."

"Yes, and then when you were born *you* almost died," my sister says. "That's why, when you finally pulled out of it they were so crazy about you and so overprotective.. and thought you were the most brilliant thing that had ever set foot on this earth... and collected your 200 first words in a scrapbook...I found it much later. By the time I was born six years later they were used to having a child so it wasn't such a big deal. They never collected my 200 first words."

"Well. First-time parents, you know, they do silly things the first time, " I say, faltering.

"Well, Dad treated you like the son he never would have, since the baby boy had died, and that's why he set you on a pedestal and talked to you all the time and bought you books and read you all that poetry at bedtime and then when you became a teenager he talked to you all the time..." My sister is growing agitated. Two bright pink spots have appeared in her cheeks.

"Maybe that's all true," I say slowly. "But I still don't think Mom minded. They had their relationship, and it had nothing to do with us and it was good. It was great."

"How could you possibly think she didn't mind how you monopolized him? How could you think she didn't mind being left out of the talks, excluded from the conversations?"

A vague feeling of guilt is starting to spread over me. Yes, it is probably true! I have always had this fantasy of my parents' happy marriage and here is my sister painting a completely different picture. A picture of a woman whose husband was stolen by a daughter. Of an unhappy woman who, though she appeared happy in public, cried a lot in private.

But had she cried? No matter how I rack my brain, I cannot remember her crying. Laughing, yes. Giggling, yes. And it's true that I, growing into young womanhood, had looked down on her a little, had not taken her very seriously. Thought of her as a little flighty. A lightweight. What a bluestocking, what a revolting young intellectual I must have been! Devaluing my mother, not appreciating her worth as a lovely, sweet, devoted woman, just because she hadn't read Proust! Always laughing...not a serious thought in her head...

But such fun! Such fun the sisters had always been! The three sisters, light of heart, light of mind! Had I truly, priggishly, devalued them? NO! I had always adored them, all of them. Just as I still adore my Aunt Florence who, right now, in the hearse on the way to her beloved sister's funeral, is telling a hilarious story of how, when her time comes, she's like to be buried with Walter on one side, Charles on the other, and Sal (her current beau) perhaps a bit down the way. No, I had never devalued, never discounted them. My sister was wrong. And I had not mistreated my mother....

Yes, I had! I had monopolized my father, ignored my mother, for many years starting in adolescence. Never let her get a word in edgewise. Never paid much attention to what she said because I figured it wasn't worth much.

And then…later…trying to make up for it all by being the "good daughter" these past few years since Dad's death… driving four hours each weekend to visit her; taking care of her accounts; and feeling virtuous and morally superior! The ultimate prig!

The hearse slows down as it enters the gravel driveway of the cemetery. I glance at my sister. I can see that, far from feeling guilty, she is suffused with anger at how I ignored and mistreated my mother over all those years. And I am feeling guilt, wave upon wave of guilt, as we stand at the grave and watch the plain wood coffin with its fragile, mysterious burden lowered into the earth.

# About the Author

Judith Davidson Chasek was an accomplished writer of short stories, journalist, and teacher. She was born in 1930 in New Jersey, the daughter of a conservative rabbi and an aspiring concert pianist. Her short stories were published in numerous magazines, including *Good Housekeeping*, *Seventeen*, and *Short Story International*. She was a reporter for the *Stamford Advocate* and the *Patent Trader*, where she particularly enjoyed her beat on the local courts. She raised two daughters with her husband Norman Chasek, an engineer and inventor, in Stamford, Connecticut, where she also became deeply involved in desegregating the local schools, voting rights, and education issues.

www.ingramcontent.com/pod-product-compliance
Lightning Source LLC
Chambersburg PA
CBHW020741130626
46554CB00006B/2096